FREE AT LAST!

For my niece Laila
and in memory of my sister Clare (May 1950-January 2009)

Noreen Mackey

Free at Last!

An Introduction to Prayer and Spirituality

the columba press

First published in 2009 by
the columba press
55A Spruce Avenue, Stillorgan Industrial Park,
Blackrock, Co Dublin

Cover by Bill Bolger
Origination by The Columba Press
Printed in Ireland by ColourBooks Ltd, Dublin

ISBN 978-1-85607-661-6

Acknowledgements
Thanks to Padraig Gleeson and Rosemary O'Loughlin, who read an
early draft of this book and made suggestions that were hugely helpful.
And thanks to my brother Liam for the title.

Note
Throughout this book, when referring to God, I follow, for convenience
and for a more readable text, the traditional practice of using masculine
pronouns. As I explain in the course of the book, masculine pronouns
are not descriptive of God, but then, neither are feminine pronouns.
Abandoning pronouns entirely results in a very cumbersome text
where the word 'God' is repeated several times in the same sentence.

Table of Contents

Free at last! Free at last!
Thank God Almighty, we are free at last!
– *Martin Luther King*

CHAPTER ONE

The Inner Voice

The first glimpse
of you – I remember –
was of something perilous
yet lovely.
You were like a source
that had no beginning,
like a spring welling up
in the eyes of oblivion.
And so perilous you seemed
and so intolerably lovely,
I thought to myself:
'It is a dream,
it is no more than that.'[1]

Think back a little. Can you recall a moment sometime in the past – maybe there was more than one such moment – when everything seemed to stand still and when, for a second, you knew what it was to be utterly happy? Perhaps it was one day in summer when you went for a walk alone. You came to the brow of a hill and were suddenly confronted with a magnificent view. For a moment, just for a moment, it was as though time had stopped, and you and nature were in perfect harmony. Or perhaps it was as you listened to some great symphony or song, and suddenly, the exultation of the music lifted you out of yourself and for an instant, you and the music were one. When it was over, it seemed to you that you had just experienced a moment of perfect happiness, and you felt a little nostalgic for a while. What had happened? Your deepest self had made itself felt, your spirit had for once pushed itself to the forefront of your consciousness and shown you what life would be like if it could be free.

I remember the first such occasion in my own life. I was sixteen, and I was walking with my father in the hills near our home in Dublin on a still, sultry August afternoon. We had turned for home, and were making our way downhill. When we reached the bottom, I looked up at the dark hills which brooded over the valley. Everything inside me was suddenly still. I forgot my father was with me, and for a moment, I seemed to forget even myself. It is a moment whose memory has never left me, even today, more than forty years later.

A friend of mine recalls a similar moment that she experienced on a Monday morning, one of those mornings that come to all of us, when she really hadn't wanted to get out of bed. A day full of problems lay ahead and she wasn't looking forward to it. Her walk to work led her past a small but picturesque cottage, one that she had often noticed before and admired in a passing way. That day was destined to be different. As she passed the cottage, she noticed the roses around the door, and stopped for a moment to look at them. At that instant, the sun's rays pierced through the cloudy sky and suddenly something about the concatenation of the cottage, the roses, the misty light and her own presence there pierced her through like an arrow. Struggling for words to explain afterwards what had happened, she said that all of these things suddenly became one, and she was one with them. There was a beautiful and totally exhilarating rightness about it all that lifted her out of herself for an instant. The whole experience was over almost before she realised it had begun, but the sweetness and happiness of it stayed with her and transformed her day.

A secret invitation

Within each of us there is something that draws us inward, into a contemplative space. In today's world, many people might find this difficult to believe. If, for example, you are the parent of a young child and you are also trying to hold down a busy job, you will be hard put to it to find time to eat, let alone indulge in contemplation. Or if you are running your own business, even your weekends may be given up to simply keeping things afloat. You will certainly not be aware of any great urge or need to stand staring into space – or whatever it is that people do when they contemplate!

Yet, you are born with the desire for something greater than yourself, something above and beyond yourself. You are born with a thirst for the immortal and the eternal. You are born with a desire to soar like an eagle above the pettiness and pain of everyday life. This desire comes suddenly to life when you least expect it – at the brow of the hill that overlooks that wonderful view, at the first swelling chords of the symphony, at the utter rightness of the little cottage in its place on a gloomy Monday morning. And until you recognise that desire and begin to look for ways to fulfil it, nothing will really satisfy you. There will always be a niggling question even during the happiest of times: is this really all there is? St Augustine put it well:

You have made us for yourself, O God,
and our hearts are restless until they rest in you.

Where has this longing come from, this desire that seems rooted in your deepest self? What if it wasn't just a desire, just a longing, but was instead a response to something or someone else? What if some deep part of you had heard a voice calling you by name, inviting you? What if someone else were active, were drawing you; and the longing you felt was an attraction towards that someone? Wouldn't that be extraordinary? Where would such an invitation lead you, if you were to accept it?

An invitation to embark upon a journey
In the Old Testament, there are a number of stories which tell of God issuing an invitation to a human. In Genesis, we read about Abraham, an old man at the time, to whom the Lord spoke one day, saying:

Go from your country and your kindred and your father's

house to the land that I will show you. I will make of you a great nation, and I will bless you and make your name great, so that you will be a blessing. I will bless those who bless you, and the one who curses you I will curse; and in you all the families of the earth shall be blessed.[2]

What would you have done in such circumstances? If you are like me, and like most of us, you would probably have thought twice about it, and then decided that it really would be most unwise at your age and state of health. And after all, health is a gift from God and he wouldn't expect you to put it at risk in a harebrained adventure of that sort. In short, you would have been sensible and mature about it. And you would have stayed at home. Abraham didn't. He got up, old as he was, and left everything that he had ever known, all his security and familiar surroundings, and set off. Something inside him drew him on and on. The call and the invitation that he had heard in his heart demanded a response. The invitation to Abraham was to set out on a journey, a journey that would end with great blessings for him.

An invitation to an encounter

In the Book of Exodus, we find the story of Moses, who was going about his ordinary business, herding the sheep of his father-in-law, Jethro, when he saw an extraordinary sight. A bush was on fire, all alone in the middle of the wilderness, and although it was burning, it was not being consumed. The bush was clothed in flame like a garment.

'I must go closer and look at this extraordinary sight', Moses said to himself.

And as he drew near, a voice spoke to him from the bush, calling him by name:

'Moses, Moses!'

And Moses responded. 'Here I am!'

Then the voice told him to remove his sandals, for he was on holy ground. The voice said:

'I am the God of your father, the God of Abraham, the God of Isaac and the God of Jacob.'[3]

This first meeting with God paved the way for a lifetime of similar encounters, each one deepening the relationship between Moses and God, and each one increasing Moses' knowledge of God, until the point came where God, as the Book of Exodus tells us, used to speak to Moses face to face, as one speaks to a friend.[4]

The invitation made to Moses at the burning bush was an invitation to an encounter, leading to a lifetime of friendship with God.

An invitation to adventure

Further on again is the story of the young Samuel, who was woken from sleep several times by a voice that called his name: 'Samuel, Samuel!' And the young boy ran to his master Eli, thinking that it was he who had called. After this had happened on a number of occasions, the wise old master guessed what was happening to the boy.

'Samuel', he said to him, 'the next time you hear your name being called, say "Speak, Lord, your servant is listening!"'

Samuel did so, the Lord responded, and for Samuel, that was the beginning of a lifetime of meetings with God.[5]

In each of the stories we have just looked at, there is one common feature. God takes the initiative. He issued the invitation. In each case, everything that followed for Abraham, Moses and Samuel was a consequence of their acceptance of God's invitation. God is a God who comes. He makes the first move towards you. The unnameable longing that afflicts you at times is the echo in your conscious mind of the voice that speaks in your deepest self, that same voice that Abraham, Moses and Samuel heard addressing them. It addresses the deepest part of you, the part where you are most truly yourself. This book is about recognising that voice, coming to realise that it requires a response, and learning, like Samuel, how to respond. Your spirit, that deepest part of you, already knows how to do this, and indeed that is its only job. But it is imprisoned, unable to communicate its wonderful discoveries to that other part of you, the conscious part. You must learn how to liberate your deepest self – or, to be more accurate, how to co-operate with God in his liberation of your deepest self – so that it can become one with you, so that you can hear with its ears and speak with its tongue.

Your hunger for love

Beginning in the 1960s, but increasing to a remarkable extent over the past twenty years, there has been a reawakening of interest in what can loosely be described as 'mind-body-spirit' matters. You have only to walk into any bookshop to see the variety of books on spirituality in one form or another that exists. There is a thriving market for such books today, as publishers have not been slow to realise. It is, I think, significant that this interest has kept pace with a general increase in prosperity and materialism, and with the gradual falling away of the values inculcated in times past by formalised religion, and with the loss of the old faiths. In the old days, people's beliefs were formed in their childhood, and rarely questioned in later life. This is not so today, and many people find themselves adrift, searching for a plank to cling to in the often stormy sea that we call 'life'. It is in this context that people are looking for meaning beyond what they can see, and for a power outside themselves that they can trust. Whether or not everybody engaged in that search realises it, they are looking for the Being that most of us call God.

There is inside each one of us an essential loneliness that no human love can assuage. This hunger, this loneliness, can be acutely painful. People have a variety of ways of dulling the pain, some more successful than others. Some fill that inner void with family, with relationships, with work. These things are often so fulfilling that while they last the people concerned no longer feel the need of something more. And it is true that human love, at its best, comes closest to what we are all seeking. But even the most perfect human love can fail you. The beloved person may die, may leave, may develop an illness of mind that takes him or her away in a different way. Work too can fail: nobody can work forever. When these events occur, people are once again brought face to face with that inner need, and they wonder what it is that can truly satisfy them.

Others fill the void in more dangerous ways: with drugs and drink and other addictions. These too dull the pain, without however giving the sense of fulfilment and enrichment that human love can offer. And of course they are dangerous to health, they can wreck relationships, they can destroy life. But in spite of this, they may in fact lead the addicted person more quickly to the truth of what it is that he or she truly needs. Sooner or later, addicted people hit a personal rock bottom where they are faced with a stark choice: to continue to hand over the control of their life to the slave-master of addiction, or to face the frightening void that will be uncovered if they give up the addictive behaviour. If they have the courage and the grace to face that void, they will discover that in it is what they have always been seeking: God.

The idea of God

So who is God? Or indeed, what is God? We can give many answers to that question. We can say that God is the Creator. We can take a phrase from the Old Testament, and say that God is 'He who is'. Or we can say that God is the Eternal One, the Holy One. But what does any of this mean? And indeed, why do we say 'he' at all? Why not 'she', or 'it'? God is not male, but then God is not female either. These are physical attributes, and God is not physical. So 'he' is not a correct pronoun, but neither is 'she', nor 'it'. The truth is, we do not know who this Being is that we call God. We use the word 'God' as if it were the given name of this Being. But of course it isn't; it is a description, in the same way that the word 'human' is not your name, or mine; it is descriptive of both of us.

Those of us who were brought up in believing families, no matter what our religion, will have formed an idea of God in our childhood. That idea will of necessity be childish. Unfortunately, although our other childish ideas will have matured as we grew to adulthood, it not infrequently happens that our idea of God

13

stays stuck at the level of that of an eight-year-old, resulting in a belief in a God who, on the one hand, has to be appeased when we have misbehaved, and on the other, might, if we behave ourselves and ask nicely, give us the things we think we need.

When I was a child, growing up in a traditionally Catholic home, my mother would warn me to be good, or 'Holy God' would be cross. Similar injunctions came from the nuns at school. So at an early stage, I formed the impression that God was something between a rather strict teacher and a policeman, constantly watching me to make sure I behaved myself. There was of course something benevolent about him too: he was pleased when I was good, and might even reward me by answering my prayers, although I was a bit disenchanted on that score after having prayed without success for several days for a pair of red sandals that I had seen in the window of Lee's Drapery Store in Rathmines, when out shopping with my mother. I looked hopefully at the end of my bed every morning, assuming that God could do the same trick as Santa Clause, and leave presents on your bed while you were asleep. But he didn't. So that was a disappointment.

God, the Lover

As I grew older, I didn't think about God too much. I said my prayers, certainly, and went to Mass on Sundays, and I avoided doing anything that might get me into serious trouble with him, but I didn't really believe any more that he had his eye on me every single minute. And then, when I was fifteen, everything changed. I stumbled upon a poem written by the great Spanish mystic and poet, St John of the Cross. It was a love poem. It told of a woman who left her house under cover of darkness to go in search of her beloved.

> On a dark night,
> Kindled in love with yearnings –
> Oh, happy chance! –
> I went forth without being observed,
> My house being now at rest.

The poem was a wonderful one, but what was most extraordinary about it to me was that, as St John of the Cross explained it, the beloved whom the woman was seeking was God.

The idea of God as a lover changed everything for me, and it is that idea of God which motivates my life to this day. To me, it means that life can be lived in relationship with God. And if the relationship is one in which God is like a lover, then it is a relationship that demands a response of love. The rest of my life has been that journey, that quest, which the poem of John of the Cross describes. It is a quest that, according to the poem, ends in a secret place where the lover and the Beloved are united in a lovers' embrace.

What an extraordinary description of our relationship with the Being we call God! If it is true, it means that you are capable of being united with God, and indeed, that is the whole thrust of St John of the Cross' writings. And he goes further. Somewhere else in his writings he says this: 'If the soul is seeking its Beloved, how much more is the Beloved seeking the soul!' Not only are you capable of union with God, but God himself is actively seeking this. God is inviting you, whether you are a husband, a wife, a lover, a child, a single person, whether you are young or old, rich or poor, to embark upon this quest, this amazing adventure, that will lead you, if only you have the courage to take up the invitation, to the very fullness of freedom, life and love. The inner voice is the voice of a lover.

Getting to know the Lover
If the loneliness and the hunger that is deep inside you is really caused by your deepest self hearing the voice of a Lover calling you by name, then surely the way to assuage that hunger and heal that loneliness is by coming to know this Lover and responding to his call. This raises two questions: first, how can you get to know him and second, why is he calling you?

Getting to know anyone demands personal contact. You cannot really get to know someone from a distance. If, for example, I read a really good biography of, say, Kingsley Amis, I will learn a great deal about him, but I won't be able to say I know him. If I then go on to read his *Memoirs*, I will discover even more about him, because in it are deeply personal and intimate revelations about himself. Yet, if a friend later said to me, 'Did you know Kingsley Amis?' I would have to admit that I didn't. If I lied and said I did, the next question my friend would probably ask would be, 'Really? Where did you meet him?' You can know a lot about another person, but you cannot actually know that person without having met him and had prolonged and close personal contact with him.

The girl who watched the film in her best friend's glasses

Think of your best friend. You know her very well, and she knows you. How did that state of things come about? When I was ten years old, we moved house and as a result my sister and I changed schools. I didn't much care for the new school at first. I didn't know anybody there, and I missed the friends I had made in my old school. Then, one day at a school film, I became aware that the girl who was sitting beside me was peering into my face instead of looking at the screen.

'What are you doing?' I hissed, out of the corner of my mouth.

'I'm watching the film in your glasses!' she whispered back.

Ever since, whenever I hear the theme music from that film, I see hovering in front of me a pale nine-year old face with a sprinkling of freckles and two prominent front teeth, eyes squinting in an attempt to follow the action reflected in my plastic-rimmed glasses. It was the beginning of a friendship that lasted through primary and secondary school, and endures to this day.

In the same way, you cannot know God without personal contact. How can you achieve this? How can you know the Unknowable? Is there a place where you can meet him? Yes, there is. Prayer is the place where God and the human being can meet in total truth, and can share with one another. Prayer is the place where the relationship grows and develops, and what you learn there will affect your life, your relationships and your work.

It takes two to pray

The word 'prayer', used in this context, may require some explanation. Like the word 'God', the word 'prayer' can be defined in many ways. It can describe what you are doing when you ask God for something, or when you thank him. Or it can describe the action of addressing him in order to praise him. But there is another kind of prayer which does not depend on any words being said by you. You are simply there, in God's presence, having set aside some time to do precisely that. If you are not addressing God in words, what is happening? God is speaking to you. Because indeed, the most important thing to remember about prayer is that it involves two parties: you – and God. We call this kind of prayer 'contemplative' prayer.

Think of some occasion recently when you decided to pray – perhaps you were passing a church and went in for a moment. You knelt or sat down – and then what happened? At a guess, I would say you began to speak to God. Did he reply? I can almost hear you saying 'Of course not!' Were you disappointed that he didn't? Again, the answer is probably 'No'. Why? I'll make another guess: because you didn't expect God to take any part in the prayer.

Reflect on that for a moment. Isn't it rather odd? Can you think of any situation in ordinary human intercourse where you would meet another person, speak to him or her at some length and then get up and leave, not in the least surprised by the fact that your friend had remained silent throughout? Yet you behave as if this was normal in prayer. But if there really is an inner voice calling you by name, is it likely that once you answer, that voice will fall silent for evermore? In the stories of the call of Abraham, Moses and Samuel, that first intervention on the part of God was, as we saw, only the beginning of a long dialogue.

Training your inner ear

Yet, if God is speaking to you in prayer, why do you not hear him? Could it possibly be that you aren't listening? The voice of God is not like a human voice. You have to train your inner ears to become attuned to the sound of that sweet and sheer silence. After all, as you've already seen, God has been calling you by name for a long time, but you misheard him. You knew something was going on, that in some vague way you were unhappy or dissatisfied, but only now are you beginning to realise that this is caused by a longing at your deepest level to respond to the Lover's voice.

Your inner senses

Talk of 'inner ears' may seem strange to you if you have not yet had the experience of inner listening. But as time goes on, and you become more at home with the sort of prayer we are talking about here, you will discover that you have inner senses that duplicate your outer senses. There is a way of hearing what cannot be heard with your bodily ears, a way of seeing what cannot be seen with your bodily eyes. There is an inner sense of touch – and indeed, if you think of that, the whole thing may begin to make more sense to you. We speak quite commonly of being deeply 'touched' by some experience – beautiful music, an unexpectedly loving gesture, the sight of a new-born baby. What do we mean when we speak of being 'touched' in this way? We mean an internal reaction, something that vibrates inside us in response to the 'touching' event. The next time it happens to you, pause for a moment to notice this inner reaction: you will find that there is a distinct sense of being physically touched in some very deep part of your being. That inner sense of touch is the one we are most familiar with because, in most people, it is the most developed of the inner senses. But you will find that with the practice of contemplative prayer, all your inner senses will gradually develop

Don't be put off by the term 'contemplative prayer', which you may imagine to be the prerogative of monks and nuns in contemplative monasteries. It is not. It is an essential part of the spiritual life for anyone who is serious about living that life. It is in the regular practice of contemplative prayer that you gradually come to know God. And when you get to know him in this deeply personal and intimate way, you will learn the secret of what it is that he has been calling you to, what it is that you are invited to.

What then is your role in this sort of prayer? It's really very simple. You just have to be still. In order to enter into this very new sort of relationship with God, you must accustom your inner senses to receive him. This is the beginning of the liberation of your deepest self.

Listening to the sound of silence

The Old Testament tells us that Elijah was instructed by God to go to Mount Horeb, where the Lord would pass by. He went and stood on the mountain, and in turn experienced a great wind, an earthquake and a fire, but the Lord was not present in any of those. Finally, there came 'a sound of sheer silence', and when Elijah heard it, he wrapped his face in his cloak, for he knew that he was in the presence of God. The scripture significantly says that Elijah 'heard' the sound of sheer silence. And it is indeed true that when your outer senses become accustomed to the stillness of prayer, your inner ear will hear what your bodily ear would perceive as silence, and your inner eyes will meet the look of love coming from the eyes of God engraved upon your inmost heart. Your inner senses are already attuned to the 'sound of sheer silence' like that in which the Lord spoke to the prophet Elijah at Horeb. Now your external senses must learn this difficult trick.

You can enter into this sort of prayer by making an act of trust in God. 'I know you are there, O Lord, and that you love me. You are there and you wish to make yourself known to me. Here I am, like Samuel. Speak, Lord, for your servant is listening.' You then simply wait. This is not easy. This is the point at which you will be assailed by all sorts of distractions. Don't let them worry you, because they quite simply don't matter. Something of great moment is going on at a level too deep for you to grasp, and your mind has to be occupied with something. But more of all of this later. For now, all you need to be aware of is that God wants this meeting much more than you do. Remember the saying of St John of the Cross: 'If the soul is seeking her beloved, how much more is her beloved seeking her!'

Removing the armour

Perhaps you remember that, back in the nineteen nineties, a nun called Sister Wendy Beckett made quite a hit on BBC television with a series of programmes on art. She became well known for her original views on famous paintings. What was less well known about her was that she was (and still is) living as a hermit in the grounds of a convent in England, where she spends six hours of every day in prayer. Recently, she wrote a book on prayer, and in it, she makes the following extraordinary statement:

> The essential act of prayer is to stand unprotected before God. What will God do? He will take possession of us.[6]

The idea that if you stand unprotected before God he will take possession of you may not be a comfortable notion, nor one that readily inspires confidence in prayer. If God takes possession of you, you might ask, what will become of your autonomy, your independence? Will you be no more than a puppet in the hands of the puppet-master? Wendy Beckett is ready with a response. That God should take possession of us is, she says, the whole purpose of life. And there you have it in a nutshell. He who would save his life must lose it. Unless the grain of wheat falls to the ground and dies, it just remains a grain of wheat. The gospels say the same thing in so many different ways, but in the end, they all come to this: the life you live is only a half-life until you are born again to live by the life of God. You are like the shades and wraiths of mythology who believed themselves to be alive when in fact they were half dead. It's true that something must die in order for you to truly come alive: the false image of yourself that you have constructed must be chopped away until there is nothing left but the true you, you as you are in your deepest depths, standing there before God in the state in which he created you. Then God can take possession of you, then God can begin to cloth the dead bones with flesh and sinews, like the dead bones in the vision of the prophet Ezekiel. Then God's breath can breathe through you, and you can begin to live the life of freedom and love that you were born to live.

God is a God who loves you unconditionally, who will not rest until he has brought you into the fullness of life and freedom that he has created you to enjoy. Your part in this doesn't necessarily involve doing exceptional things, or living some extraordinary way of life. It simply means letting God be God – giving up some time in your day just to be totally present to him, to stand unprotected before him. And then you will see the wonderful things he will do in your life.

Why is God calling you?
If, until now, you have never really prayed, or, more likely, prayed only when you wanted something, you will be more at ease with the idea that you call upon God, rather than that God calls you. You might by now be feeling a little puzzled. Why would God be calling you? What could he want with you, or need from you? Isn't he all powerful, totally sufficient to himself? Well, yes, and no.

Yes, we know that God is all-powerful. But we also know that God is love.[7] If God is actually love, rather than simply loving, then God's nature must be the nature of love. And love needs to give; that is its essential quality. Love lives in and for the other. So it is that we have been created so that God can fulfil his need of giving, of living in us and for us. And what is it that God will give us? He will give us life. God is life-giving, and all his plans are made in order that we should have the fullness of life and freedom. Jesus himself has told us this: 'I have come that they may have life, and have it to the full.'

CHAPTER TWO

Setting Out on the Journey

Now all this is very well, you may say, but what exactly is it I am to do? How do I embark upon this way of praying, a way that seems very different from what I'm used to? You may have even tried this before, and given up in despair after days or weeks in which all you seemed to be doing was wool-gathering. Well, perhaps you are wrong: perhaps you weren't wool-gathering at all, but I'll say something about that later. For the moment, let's suppose that either you've never tried this before, or that somehow or other it seemed more difficult than it is.

Thinking of your body

The first thing you need to do is to remind yourself that you are not an angel – in other words, you have a body as well as a spirit. Your spirit may be totally at home with contemplative prayer, but your body is not. You have to bring it along too, so you need to remember that it must be comfortable and at ease with what is going on. Since your spirit needs less encouragement to begin, you should at the start concentrate on your body. This means thinking of a place, a time and a posture that will make your body feel that all is well, and that will help it to relax into what is going on – without of course relaxing so much that you fall asleep!

Finding a place

First, you need to find a place. Like all of us, you are a creature of habit, and to a large extent, you are conditioned by your surroundings. You find it much easier to settle down to your daily work when you reach your desk at the office than you do when you bring some files home, for example. At home, you have distractions that you don't have in the office. The children interrupt you, a friend telephones, someone calls to the door. It's the same with prayer. If you try to pray sitting at the kitchen table, you will suddenly notice that loose knob on the cupboard door. Might as well fix that now while you have the time, it will only take a minute. There. That's done. Now to begin the prayer. Goodness, you never noticed that mark on the table before. What idiot put a hot cup down there? If you've told them once, you've told them a hundred times to use a coaster. Well, thank goodness you have that brilliant new product that removes marks from furniture with a simple rub of a cloth. Now where did you put it? Oh yes, here it is. Just dab it on, like so ... Now, a quick energetic rub and, hey presto! The mark is gone. Wonderful stuff! Wonder if there are marks on other pieces of furniture that you could remove while you're at it? You go on a watermark hunt and find a few more around the house. Finally, a half hour later the furniture is in pristine condition, but oh dear, what has happened to your prayer time? You get the picture.

What is necessary is to have a place that is devoted – or almost devoted – to prayer. If you have the luxury of an entire room for this purpose, wonderful. Most people won't, so the next best thing is to have a corner. Ideally, it should be a corner of a room that is not in constant use by every other member of the family. Your bedroom would be a good place.

In my own case, as I live alone, I am lucky enough to be able to use the guest bedroom for this purpose. However, since occasionally a friend comes to visit, I can't turn it totally into an oratory, so I keep a sofa bed there, which can be opened out when necessary. During the rest of the time, it is my place for prayer, and when I close the door behind me there is nothing in the room that recalls any other activity. Many years ago, when I lived in a small apartment, an alcove in the entrance hallway was my prayer room. Be inventive. You will be surprised how many unused corners there are in your home.

But whether you have an entire room or just a corner of a room at your disposal, the essential thing is to turn it into a sacred space. You can do this in any way that is pleasing to your own eyes. Some people like simplicity, others prefer more detailed decoration. Either way, it should be significant to you as a space in which you will meet God.

You could, for example, simply place an icon or other sacred image on a table, together with a candle. Or instead of the icon, you could use a cross, or a copy of the Bible. Ideally, you would leave these there permanently (or as permanently as possible: when a friend comes to stay in my guestroom I remove my sacred space, but leave it there at all other times.) But try to avoid dismantling the space every time you finish your time of prayer, as its permanence will serve as a reminder to you, and will also consecrate that particular place in your house so that when you enter it you will not be distracted by the thoughts of whatever other use the space is put to outside prayer. But don't worry if for whatever reason it is impossible to leave it there between prayer periods: God, your Lover, who is longing to meet you, is not going to allow a little thing like that to prevent it. In fact, at this point I want to say something very important. God is not going to allow *anything* to prevent your meeting, if you yourself want to meet God. So even if there is nowhere in your home that you can turn into a sacred space – indeed, even if you have no home at all – you can create an inner sacred space simply by closing your eyes and recalling that God is there, present with you.

Making time

When you have decided upon and arranged your sacred space, (outer or inner) choose the time that will be dedicated to prayer every day. Do this, even if you know you will not always be able to stick to it. If you don't fix a time, there is a strong chance that the entire practice will simply fall by the wayside.

Sometimes, a box of tablets contains the following instruction: 'Take one at the same time each day. If you miss a day, just take one again the following day.' This is an excellent instruction for prayer. If you miss a day – or even more than a day – then let there be no panic, to use a favourite expression of my father's. Just begin again at the same time the following day.

When choosing a time, it's important to have regard to two things: your body clock and the likelihood of being disturbed. If you are a morning person, then that is the best time for prayer, as you are more likely to fall asleep if you try to pray in the evenings. On the other hand, if you have small children, then the optimal time will probably be after they have gone to bed. Decide what is best for you, and then decide how long it is going to be. This will depend very much on how busy your life is, but one thing is certain: if you want to make time for prayer, you will do so. If you can devote an hour, that is an ideal amount of time. But if all you can manage is ten minutes, then decide to devote ten minutes.

I have a friend who is the mother of a family. One of her children is profoundly disabled. This friend of mine has practically no time to call her own, yet she prays for at least an hour every day. She finds this time because she wants to; prayer to her is as necessary as eating and sleeping. It colours her whole life, and through it she has come to know profound truths about the meaning of her own life and that of her disabled daughter. It was during prayer that she realised that her daughter was absolutely perfect to God, and it was through prayer too that she came to an awareness that allows her to see the gifts her daughter has to offer, like her ability to love unconditionally.

My friend knows that she needs constant prayer to keep her aware of the value of her daughter's life, to value what is weakest in the community, to be content to live a hidden life, a life that many people would see as a waste, although she knows it is not. She knows that God is there, precisely in the ordinary basic living, in the struggle to get up at night to attend to her daughter, in the powerlessness that she so often experiences as she watches her suffer. And she knows that God is also in the joy she feels in the delight her daughter manifests when she sees her mother during the night, which my friend believes mirrors the response God has for each one of us when we turn to him.

So decide what time you can make available to God, whether it's ten minutes or an hour, and stick to that except when through one of the unavoidable circumstances that occur in the life of each of us, you have to curtail it or miss it entirely.

Getting comfortable

Having chosen your space and your time, the final thing needed to make your body feel at home is posture. Gone are the days when Christians considered they weren't praying unless they were on their knees! That's not to say that it isn't good to kneel to pray – indeed it is. It is a reverent attitude, and helps to put you in an attitude which both reminds you of the transcendence of the One to whom you are praying and adjusts your relationship with him. So it is that we kneel at moments of particular mystery, such as the consecration of the Mass. It is good too to begin your period of prayer in a kneeling attitude, and to return to it for a few moments at the end.

But what we are now considering is the posture you should adopt for the main part of your prayer period. Ideally, it will be a posture which, while comfortable, and not causing you to be unduly distracted by aches and itches, will at the same time enable you to remain alert. Here there is much to be learnt from eastern traditions. The lotus position, for those who are physically flexible enough to adopt it, is ideal. Next best is a prayer stool, which allows you to sit back on your heels with the support of the stool under your buttocks.

For those of you who are unable to bend your limbs into the positions necessary for either the lotus or the prayer stool, the best alternative is to sit on an upright chair, back straight and supported, feet firmly on the ground, hands in the lap, either loosely clasped or open. Don't slouch! If you slouch, you will almost certainly fall asleep.

So there you are. Your sacred space is ready, the hour you have chosen has come, your chair or prayer stool awaits you.

Now light the candle in your sacred space to symbolise the presence of the Other you have come to meet. You are ready to begin.

What do you do now?

Focusing

Remember first of all that a deep part of you is at home with this: your deepest self has been doing this all your life. You are now starting to set it free to engage the whole of you in this journey that is about to begin.

Kneel for a few moments and recall why you are there: you are there to spend a short time with God, who is there with you, who knows all about you, who loves you more than you could ever imagine and who wants above all to lead you into freedom and into life. It is a good idea to begin and end with some short formal prayer: this helps to shape the period. The opening prayer focuses the mind, and the closing prayer brings you back, at least at the end, to why you are there. For myself, I always begin with a prayer to the Holy Spirit, asking for the Spirit's guidance and light. I usually end with the prayer of Charles de Foucauld: 'Father, I abandon myself to you.' A very good prayer to end with is the Our Father.

After your opening prayer, whatever it is, tell God that you are there for him, that this time is purely for him. Tell him that no matter how bored you may feel during the period you have decided upon, you will not walk away from it. If you can do no more, you can at least 'waste' this time, put it beyond any other use that you might make of it. The next ten or fifteen or sixty minutes will be like the perfumed ointment that Mary of Bethany poured over the feet of Jesus, a seeming waste to those who were present, but to Jesus, an act of love.[8]

Ask him to open your inner ears to his words, and to open your heart to receive them, so that you will be able to be open to whatever it is he is calling you to. 'You are there, O Lord, my Father and my Love. You are there and you wish to make yourself known to me.' Then adopt whatever posture is best for you –

lotus, sitting on a prayer stool, or sitting on a straight-backed chair. It's up to you.

This is the point at which people begin to feel at a loss. It is difficult, when you have not been used to it, to pray without using set prayers like the Our Father or the Hail Mary, or some other prayer that you have been accustomed to read. What you are doing here is trying to get your conscious mind accustomed to something that your deepest self has been doing all your life – being in God's presence, talking to him and learning from him. For there are two present at this meeting: you and God, and God will not simply be there like an inanimate object. He will be active, always about his business of guiding you along the road to freedom and to life.

Learning to be present

When I was a child, a big feature of our Sunday afternoons at home was The Maureen Potter Show on the radio. Various catch-phrases from the show, such as 'Hignore him, Hignatius', became part of our family vocabulary. One such catch-phrase, used regularly by the great Maureen in respect of a chronically absent-minded character in the show was 'Ah, he's not with us!' This is a phrase that describes most of us most of the time. We are very rarely fully among those present. We are very rarely totally present to anything. Our body is there certainly, but our minds are either in the past, occupied with reliving past pleasures, or with regrets, or they have leaped ahead to a future we do not possess, planning, worrying, wondering. As soon as you sit back and try to be silent, you will become painfully aware of this dispersion of your self.

But prayer demands your presence. It is, after all, a meeting between friends. If you were meeting a human friend it would be a strange thing if you were there only in body, but your mind was elsewhere. Therefore, the first thing you will need to do is learn how to be present.

There are various techniques for calming and focusing the mind at the beginning of prayer, and it is a question of experi-

menting until you find the one that best suits your temperament. We will take three examples here. The first is unique to the
Christian tradition; the other two are common to most traditions
of prayer and meditation.

Imaginative use of scripture

The first is an imaginative exercise in which you choose some
scene from the scriptures – for example, the birth of Jesus – and
you place yourself in the scene, either as one of the participants,
or as yourself. For example, you might choose to be Joseph. You
imagine yourself there in the cave at Bethlehem where Mary has
just given birth to Jesus, and you imagine your sensations and
emotions: fear for this new-born baby in such harsh, unwelcom-
ing conditions; a sense of responsibility, perhaps. Or you could
imagine yourself exactly as you are, but transported into that
scene and made a part of it. Mary and Joseph are aware of your
presence. What do they say to you? What do you say to them?
You may find yourself telling the child Jesus about your con-
cerns, or asking him to help you with something. Feel absolutely
free to do whatever you feel inclined. The whole purpose of this
exercise is to enable you to enter into communication with God.
You can do this exercise with any passage of scripture that ap-
peals to you. This is an excellent method for those who are able
to use their imagination in this way, but not everyone will be
able to. If you are not one of those people, then one of the methods which follow may suit you.

Following the breath

An ancient practice for helping to still the mind in preparation
for meditation or prayer is the practice known as following the
breath. Become aware of your breathing. Listen to it, but don't
interfere with it. Try to let it continue exactly as it is. Just follow
it with your mind – in, out, in, out, in, out. Gradually it will slow
down and your mind will quieten. When your mind has quiet-
ened a little, become aware of background sounds: sounds outside, birds, traffic, then sounds in the house, voices, doors closing,

pipes gurgling, the infinitesimal sounds a house makes even when nobody is there. This helps to ground you in the present. Now that you are present, recall who it is that is there with you. Now look at yourself for a moment. How are you feeling? Happy? Sad? Angry? Are you carrying some emotional baggage – perhaps you have just exchanged some heated words with someone? Perhaps you are ill, or in pain? However you are, however you feel, just tell God about it. Tell him how you feel. If you would rather be anywhere but there, tell him that too. If you are in a state of sin, tell him, like the tax collector in the gospel who then went away at rights with God.[9] The essential thing is to be totally honest, utterly truthful. You are in the one place in the entire world where you can be yourself without any fear of the consequences. You are with the one person who knows you through and through, who knows you much better than you know yourself.

Whenever you become aware that your mind has dragged you away from the present, into the past or the future, just quietly go back to following your breath again. Your breathing is in the present; God's activity in your innermost being is in the present, you want to be present to him. You are creating a space and an awareness into which he will be able to enter.

The sacred word
Another method for bringing yourself into the present and holding you there is the increasingly popular method known as Centering Prayer. You choose a word – called the sacred word, because its purpose is to remind you of the sacred reason you are there. It can be anything: God, Love, Jesus – anything you like, so long as it is not inappropriate. Once you have chosen it, however, you should stick with it; otherwise looking for new words will become a distraction. You use the sacred word in much the same way that you used your breathing in the previous example: that is, when you first sit down, you concentrate on it for a few minutes until your mind quietens, then you let it go, and enter into communication with God, telling him how

you are feeling as in the previous example. When I say 'concentrate on it', I don't mean analyse it in any way; simply set it gently before your mind. Some people like to visualise the word, others like to imagine the sound of it. Do whatever suits you best. The idea is to give your mind something to occupy it in the present moment. If you find yourself thinking about the meaning of the word, stop, and very gently go back to simply looking at it or listening to it until you quieten again. Then let it go. Like the breathing exercise, you return gently to the sacred word whenever you find yourself drawn away into the past or the future.

Listening

Up to this, the conversation between you and God has been one-way: you have been doing all the talking. But prayer is a two-way conversation, so you must also listen to God. Listening in the context of prayer requires slightly different skills from those you use normally when listening. You have to become accustomed to using your inner ear – to 'listening with your heart'.

At first, this will require a little effort on your part, but later, as we will see, it will become almost second nature, and later again, it will become your main occupation during prayer.

When you have spoken a little to God, when you have told him how you are feeling, you will probably find that one thing will lead to another. Telling God how you are feeling in a completely uninhibited, utterly truthful way may set free some emotions. You may find yourself in tears, or you may find yourself arguing with God, or remonstrating with him. Or indeed you may find yourself thanking him for something you are only now realising he has given you. But whether or not your conversation with God leads to this, at some stage during your allotted prayer it is good to introduce a short silent space. This is the space in which you are simply there for God, in case he wishes to tell you something. You may not be aware until after your prayer that you have learned something during this silent time, so it is important not to be impatient, or to go back to talking to God too quickly. Give God time. When your mind wanders, as it will, then just remind yourself gently that you are there with God.

As you gradually become more used to this way of praying, and as your inner ear becomes accustomed to listening, you may notice a development. After you have spent a short time in your focusing exercise, whether it is meditation on a scene from scripture, following the breath or using a sacred word, you may become aware of a subtle drawing or spiralling movement inward. You may feel inclined to close your eyes and just remain wrapped in peace. You may also have a subtle sense of being in some way occupied during this time – or at the very least, you will not have a desire to be doing anything else.

If you have this experience, go with it, for it means that your inner ear has become accustomed to its natural atmosphere, which is silence. And in that silence, God is speaking to you and teaching you.

This period of silent peace – or, if you prefer, of peaceful listening – will probably not last more than a couple of minutes at first. When it ends, don't try to force it. Just go back either to your focusing exercise or to speaking to God, whichever attracts you most. Then the next time you feel drawn inwards, stop, and rest again in the silence. As time goes on, these periods of silence may become both more frequent, and longer. This is good. Just go with it. We will look at this in more depth further on.

Ending
When the period you have decided upon is over, thank God for the way in which the period has passed. If it has been peaceful and happy for you, thank God for that. If it has not, if it has been boring or painful or distracted, thank him anyway, and trust that in spite of everything you have been feeling, he has been there, communicating with you at the deepest level. You have done your part: you have given up the time to him, you have put it beyond all other use to yourself. Then say whatever closing prayer you have decided upon.

CHAPTER THREE

What to Expect

What can you expect to happen as you gradually become accustomed to this way of praying? Well, many things may happen at different times, in the sense that you may experience certain things – peace, joy, love – or you may find yourself distracted, bored, or even sad. These events will often depend upon your personality, your state of health and your frame of mind. Or they may be a direct reflection of something going on in your deepest centre – that place where you are at one with God.

Awakening to the truth

But there is one thing that will certainly happen, sooner or later. You will begin to live in the truth. This is the whole purpose of the contemplative life, because it is God's own purpose for you. In the gospel of John, there is a moment where Jesus turns to the Jews who believed in him and says: 'If you continue in my word, you are truly my disciples, and you will know the truth, and the truth will make you free.'[10] The Jews misunderstood him, and objected to the implication that they were unfree. They pointed out that they had never been slaves, and asked him what he meant. Jesus answered that everyone who commits sin is a slave to sin.

God's desire for you is that you should be free. You can only be free when you live in the truth. And at an early stage in your practice of contemplative prayer, you will begin to become painfully aware that you are not living in the truth.

When some people have been practising this way of prayer for a while – it may be weeks or it may be months – a strange phenomenon takes place. The word 'truth' begins to exercise an extraordinary fascination over them. I was living in Luxembourg when this began to happen to me. Because I was speaking and thinking in French at the time, it was the French word for truth – *verité* – which began to attract me. It started to leap out at me from books, newspapers, radio and television, and each time this happened, my heart gave a strange little responsive leap, as though it had recognised an old friend. I began to ask God during prayer to lead me into the truth. I wasn't at all sure what I meant by that, but I began to feel a growing desire for truth above all things.

Anna, a woman who sometimes shares her own spiritual journey with me, speaks about a similar experience, and indeed I have noticed myself how she reacts to the word 'truth' when it comes up in our conversation. She welcomes it, again as one who welcomes an old friend.

The universal delusion

What is happening here? To answer that question, we need to look at an insight that is common to all the great religions: Something is radically wrong with human consciousness, and as a result, the normal state of the human mind is dysfunctional. Different traditions describe this dysfunction in different ways: the Christian tradition speaks of 'original sin', and those of us who were reared on the old catechism will remember that it described the effects of original sin on the human condition in this way: 'Our intellect is darkened, our will is weakened, our passions incline us to evil and we are subject to sickness and death.' Buddhism teaches that the normal state of the human mind is one that generates misery, while the Hindu tradition speaks of a normal human state of delusion.

What is this delusion? What is it that veils our understanding? What is it that generates misery? A great spiritual teacher and prophet of our times, Eckhart Tolle, says that it is precisely our belief that we are separate, our inability to see that we are part of one great unity.[11] This delusion causes you to look for your happiness in things outside yourself, whereas happiness, peace and contentment can only be found within. Many people spend their lives fighting: fighting to win happiness and fighting to resist unhappiness. And this very resistance to what they wrongly perceive as the enemy causes them more unhappiness, because they cannot control the flow of events. They live their lives, for the most part, in an unconsciousness of the great reality of their union with God and with all things. This is their delusion, this is the lie in which they live. When you emerge into the truth and live your life in it, you discover that you are free. You no longer resist, because you recognise that your place in the great order of things is the right one. When that happens, you know yourself to be the child of a loving Father, and you open your arms in full and free acceptance of both life and death, knowing that nothing can harm you. That is what Jesus meant when he said that the truth would make you free.

Three ways to truth

How does your practice of contemplative prayer lead you into this truth? It does so, I believe, in three ways. First, it puts you in deliberate and conscious contact with the Risen Jesus, who is the Way, the Truth and the Life. Second, it opens you up to the action of the Holy Spirit who, as Jesus has told us, is the Spirit of Truth. And third, it leads you into another dimension of consciousness, where you become aware of yourself as something more and greater than your thoughts and emotions, as a vast space in which thoughts and emotions take place, as a Watcher who witnesses the thoughts and emotions as they occur. You come gradually to the realisation that you are not your thoughts and emotions, and that they have no power over you.

As time goes on, and you become more accustomed to this way of praying, moments of realisation and insight – or enlightenment, to use the Buddhist term – of this kind, can come to you when you are least expecting them. In his book *Conjectures of a Guilty Bystander* the American monk and writer, Thomas Merton, describes a moment when he stood at a busy intersection in Louisville, Kentucky, and realised that he was one with all the people hurrying past in every direction. It was a moment of great joy, a moment when he saw straight into the truth of life.

A few years ago, I was on a train travelling from Charleroi to Namur in Belgium. I had a window seat, and was gazing idly out at the passing scenery when without any warning there was a sudden shift in my consciousness. I remember that I was looking at the time at an outcrop of rock when it became invested with extraordinary significance. Taken aback, I tore my gaze away. My eyes fastened on a clump of trees crowning a distant hill. They suddenly thrilled me. Then a little stony path through a field filled me with delight. It was like the dawn chorus, when first one bird, then two and then every bird within hearing begins to pour out its heart, only here the music was coming from all creation. One by one, hills, rivers, trees, stones rose up and began to sing. Everything was one and everything was in One, and I was caught up in it all somehow … for I was no longer aware of myself as in any way separate from the paean of praise that was pouring out all around me. Every bush was burning, the hills leaped like rams before the Lord of heaven and earth; the morning stars sang together and all heavenly beings shouted for joy.

I left the train at Namur to change for Luxembourg. I was bewildered and intoxicated. It can't continue, I thought; it's too good to be true. But all the way to Luxembourg the great symphony went on. As the train climbed through the Ardennes we reached the snowline and I had never seen snow like this before, snow which so exulted in its snow-ness. Everything was in its rightful place and everything rejoiced to be there. The Beloved had revealed his eyes to all his creation. He had looked at them as he passed and by his glance alone left them clothed in beauty.

We have all had moments in our lives when we were forcibly pulled out of ourselves and our habitual way of seeing things. I spoke of some of these moments at the beginning of this book. Sadly, we often forget them again almost immediately, and lapse back into the falsehood of our normal consciousness.

A shift in consciousness

However, when you regularly practice contemplative prayer, these shifts in your consciousness become more frequent, you become more aware of them and and you become more conscious of their significance. Little by little, the truth that you are experiencing begins to affect the way you live. Your relationships with other people take on greater meaning as you realise the connectedness that exists between you and other people. You begin to see that difficult people are not really difficult at all in the true essence of themselves: they simply have not entered the truth and are living in the only way that is possible for them in the circumstances. You realise that this is not how they truly are.

Your relationship with the environment also changes, as you begin to see the unity of all matter, and realise that harm done to the environment is harm done to all creation, including yourself.

You begin to learn that you can trust God, for this is also a part of the truth. You make your peace with life. You stop fighting, you stop resisting, because you know that you are safe here and now, in this present moment. You stop regretting the past, which is gone, which no longer has reality. You cease to fear the future, because again you know that the truth is that all you have is now, this present moment, and that whatever this moment holds for you is the right thing in the great scheme of things. You begin to know the peace that passes understanding. You come to understand the prayer of Jesus for his disciples at the Last Supper:

> Father, sanctify them in the truth; your word is truth. The glory that you have given me I have given them, so that they may be one as we are one. I in them and you in me, that they may be completely one, so that the world may know that you have sent me and have loved them even as you have loved me.[12]

Overflow

Every time you pray, something happens, although often it will seem to you like one big non-event. But something always happens, because God is one of the participants, and God never ceases his creative action – in your prayer just as in all creation. 'My Father is still working and I also am working', Jesus said to the Jews who complained that he was healing on the Sabbath.[13] God is forever recreating you, bringing you forth again and again into increased fullness of life, liberating you from the chains that even you were unaware of. This secret activity is constantly in train in your inmost being, that place where God is. Mostly it remains secret, but sometimes, some people get glimpses of it in one way or another. When echoes or reflections of God's secret activity spill into your conscious mind, either during or outside prayer, we call this 'overflow'.

Not everyone experiences overflow. Why does this happen to some people but not to others? We don't really know. In some cases, it may be that a person has an especially sensitive temperament, which intuits what is going on and reflects it into the conscious mind. In other cases, it may be that God sees that someone needs conscious awareness of what is going on, in order to help and encourage him or her in a difficult time. Or perhaps, where people have special roles as spiritual leaders or teachers, it is necessary for them to be able, as it were, to 'see' what is going on within them. Whatever the reason, it is important to realise one thing: the same things are happening in the depths of all people who are living a spiritual life: some can see it and some cannot. That does not in any way make the 'seers' better people.

In her book *Guidelines for Mystical Prayer*, Ruth Burrows distinguishes between what she calls 'lights on' and 'lights off' contemplatives. The 'lights on' people are those who experience overflow, who can 'see' – at least some of the time – the mysterious action of God within them. The 'lights off' people are those who cannot see what is happening – they are in the dark. But the point that Burrows makes is that both sorts of people are contemplatives and mystics, and the 'lights on' people are in no way superior, or somehow 'holier' than the others.

I now want to look at some of the forms of overflow that can be experienced.

Images

Overflow can take many forms. It may, for example, take the form of an image, or vision, where some profound event at the depths of your being presents itself to your imagination in a visual way – a little like dreams do when you are asleep.

So, for example, a profound experience of God's unconditional love may present itself to your mind as an image of Jesus embracing you. Or it may translate in a different way entirely, and the image might be one of a river flowing into a swelling sea. And so on.

You need to recognise that if images of this kind occur, the fact of their occurrence is not important. They do not make your prayer either better or worse. What is important about them is the truth they signify or symbolise. Some people lay great store by their 'visions', but if you do that, you run the risk of creating a new prison for yourself, just when God is freeing you from your old ones. An attachment to anything, even 'holy' things like visions, is an attachment to something that is not God, and is therefore an obstacle between you and God. It creates the very real risk that you will go to prayer in much the same way that people go to the cinema: to be entertained.

There is a further danger in giving undue importance to such occurrences, and that is, that if you have a very vivid imagination, it is possible to persuade yourself that you have 'seen' something 'holy'. It has happened that people have then further persuaded themselves that in consequence, they themselves must in some way be 'holy', a dangerous belief, leading as it does down a path in direct opposition to the path of truth. 'No one is good but God alone',[14] Jesus said, and it is salutary for all of us to recall those words from time to time.

Words

Overflow can also occur in the form of words, spoken somewhere deep inside us. Such words can have a quite extraordinary effect, and can actually produce the result they seem to be directed at. Traditionally, the great Christian mystics were familiar with this sort of overflow, which they called 'locutions'. In her autobiography, the sixteenth century Carmelite mystic St Teresa of Avila gives many examples of her own experiences of locutions. In one case, she tells us, the words 'Do not be afraid' spoken in the depths of her being immediately banished all the fear and anxiety that she had been suffering, and filled her with courage.

Some people may experience the hearing of inner words only once in their entire lives; others experience them regularly. And of course, as I said at the start of this section, many people never have an experience of this kind at all. An elderly French woman of my acquaintance, who had lived a deeply spiritual life for almost her entire adulthood, had one single experience, but she has never forgotten it. She was already in her seventies when it occurred, and she was travelling by train at the time. Suddenly, she heard from deep inside her a voice say, 'Cecile, I have loved you with an everlasting love.' She was completely shaken, because she had no doubt about the precise words that were used, including her name, but yet she knew that she hadn't heard them with her ears. As she said to me some time later when she was telling me the story, 'I didn't know it was possible to hear actual words without using your ears!'

Inner experiences
It is also possible for overflow to take another form, one which is notoriously difficult to describe. It is an experience where you 'see' something, but without any image presenting itself either to your physical eyes or to your mind.

In her autobiography, St Teresa of Avila describes one such occurrence in her own life. She suddenly became aware that Jesus was beside her, but she saw nothing. The experience alarmed her, because like Cecile above, she didn't know it was possible. How did she know Jesus was beside her if she neither saw him nor heard him? St Teresa was very fond of consulting what she called 'learned men' when faced with a spiritual difficulty that she was unable to resolve for herself. She did so on this occasion. The priest she consulted hadn't the faintest notion what she was talking about. He asked her how she knew it was Jesus. What did he look like? She was unable to say. What was he wearing? She couldn't answer that either. After her interview with her learned man, she was even more confused and disturbed than before. Finally, she chanced to meet with another of the many Spanish saints of the sixteenth century, the Franciscan, Peter of Alcantara, and she asked him about it. He understood and reassured her about it. Later Teresa learned that this sort of experience was called an intellectual vision. She describes it in this way:

> If someone I had never seen or heard about were to come and speak to me when I was blind or in thick darkness and were to tell me who he was, I should believe him, but I should not be able to affirm that he was that person as positively as if I had seen him. But here one can, for though He is unseen He imprints so clear a knowledge on the soul that there seems to be no possibility of doubt. The Lord is pleased to engrave it so deeply on the understanding that one can no more doubt it than one can doubt the evidence of one's eyes. In fact it is easier to doubt one's eyes. For sometimes we wonder whether we have not imagined something seen, whereas here, though that suspicion may arise momentarily, so great a certainty remains behind that the doubt has no validity.

It is possible in this way to experience profound spiritual truths, such as the indwelling of God, or the mystery of the Trinity. When the experience is over, it is impossible to recapture it, but the certainty of its having occurred lasts for many years – perhaps for a whole lifetime. It is, as St Teresa says, impossible to doubt the truth of what has occurred. So, if, for example, your experience has been one of God's presence at the very centre of your being, you will in some way have 'seen' this (without, of course having actually seen anything at all), and although you will not afterwards be able to recapture the experience, you will not be able to doubt that you knew God was there in the depths of your being.

This may all seem rather obscure, unless you have experienced it yourself. It might help if I offer an example of my own, which I have already recounted in more detail elsewhere. One day during my usual prayer time, the following verse from a poem of St John of the Cross came suddenly and without prior consideration into my mind:

O crystalline fount, If on that thy silvered surface,
Thou wouldst of a sudden form the eyes desired,
Which I bear outlined in my inmost parts.[15]

In his commentary on this verse, St John of the Cross explains that the 'eyes desired' are the eyes of the God, desired by the person who is seeking him. The crystalline fount is a metaphor for faith, and the person seeking God is asking to be allowed to see those eyes which faith tells her are engraved in her inmost being.

At the same moment that this verse came unbidden into my mind, I knew with absolute certainty that those eyes of God were indeed 'outlined in my inmost parts'. I was as aware, for one moment, of those eyes looking at me as if I were physically gazing at them. But I saw nothing. I have never been able to relive that experience, but neither have I ever been able to doubt that it happened, nor have I been able to doubt that it was an experience of something that was utterly true.

CHAPTER FOUR

Patterns in Prayer

Your prayer is totally personal to you – and, of course, to God. There are as many different ways of praying as there are people on the planet. You will relate to God in a way that is different from anyone else, because you are your unique self. For that reason, it is not a good thing to compare your prayer with that of somebody else, or to wonder why it's seemingly so easy for them and so difficult for you. You are you, and the other person is who he or she is.

The castle, the night and the islands
Having said that, the development of contemplative prayer follows, in everyone, a certain pattern, and undergoes certain predictable variations. This pattern has been recognised by all the great spiritual teachers, although each has had his or her own way of describing it. For St Teresa of Avila, prayer is a journey through a castle containing seven rooms, the first rooms being on the outside, while gradually, the praying person penetrates the inner rooms one by one, until finally reaching the seventh room, where the King lives.[16] St John of the Cross speaks, somewhat alarmingly, of a passage through a series of nights,[17] while a spiritual teacher of our own day, Ruth Burrows, prefers the metaphor of three islands.[18]

However you prefer to describe it, your prayer life, like your physical life, will go through three main stages: an early stage that resembles physical infancy, an intermediate stage that can be compared to the period in our lives that begins with childhood and ends with middle age, and finally, a stage of maturity.

Standing on the rock

I have no children of my own, but I became an aunt for the first time at an age when most of my contemporaries were becoming grandparents. My little niece Laila is an unending source of delight and amazement to all of us, as we watch her turn from a tiny newborn baby into a little person with a personality all her own. But to me, one of the most marvellous things about the whole event was to see the way in which her parents devoted their entire selves to ensuring her happiness and security in the new experience of living outside the womb. Nothing was too much trouble for them so long as Laila felt happy and wanted in her new life. So she got lots of cuddles and attention and warmth and comforting milk, and no doubt she came to the conclusion in her baby mind that things weren't so bad outside, after all.

The first stage of your prayer life will be a little like that. This is, for you, a totally new way of living. It will feel a little strange. You will be exercising inner muscles that you didn't know you had, and like my niece Laila, your movements will at first be unco-ordinated. All of this would probably make you feel so uncomfortable that you would give the whole thing up, were it not that you have a parent whose sole aim during this period is to ease you into your new life with as little disturbance as possible. God who, as Jesus has told us, is our caring father, seems to give special attention and care to those setting out in the spiritual life.

I mentioned above the images of the castle, the nights and the three islands, employed by three spiritual teachers to describe the different stages of prayer. Another image, one that has spoken to me for quite a while now, is taken from the Old Testament. It is the image of Moses standing on a rock while God passed by. The story goes that Moses asked God to show himself to him. God replied that he would do what Moses asked, because he was his friend. However, said God to Moses, I will not show you my face, because no one can see the face of God and remain alive. He said:

See, there is a place by me where you shall stand on the

rock, and while my glory passes by I will put you in a cleft
of the rock, and I will cover you with my hand until I have
passed by; then I will take away my hand, and you shall
see my back; but my face shall not be seen.[19]

When you begin your life of prayer, you will employ, as we
have seen, some method such as meditation, or following the
breath, or the sacred word, for quieting you and leading you
into inner silence. This requires effort, so you are a little like
Moses climbing up onto that rock to stand there, in a place near
God. This is the part of the work that you have to do yourself.
There is a lot of energy involved in climbing onto that rock.
Moses was an old man when this happened: rock-climbing can't
have come easily to him!

This is the stage where you are establishing a daily routine of
prayer, trying to stick to it, trying to get accustomed to meditating, to following the breath, to using a sacred word. But once
you have grown accustomed to the new routine and whatever
method you have chosen for quietening yourself, once you are
finally standing on the rock, what happens?

Experience during prayer
A number of things can be said about the rock that you are now
standing upon. First, it lifts you high above the earth and, as you
look around, you have a marvellous view. Fields and woods and
towns are all seen in their proper place as part of a whole. So it is
that in the early days of your prayer, you may find yourself lifted
up above the things that bother you, above all your usual worries and anxieties. You can often, from this vantage point, put
them in perspective. This brings you a sense of great peace,
which you will be conscious of even in the middle of your ordinary occupations.

Next, the rock is in the open air; you feel you can really
breathe and open your inner lungs. Prayer becomes your natural
atmosphere (indeed, it always was the natural atmosphere of
your deepest self; you simply hadn't been aware of it). You will
find that you are relaxing into it, and you are getting a lot of

pleasure and satisfaction from whatever you have chosen as your quietening method. This new ease even has physical repercussions: you will find your breathing becoming slower and calmer, the physical symptoms of stress or anxiety will ease; quite often, people with high blood pressure find that their blood pressure drops.

And then, of course, the most important thing about the rock that you are standing on is that it is in a place that is near God. Often in the early months and years of your practice of this form of prayer, the awareness of that nearness of God will give you a sense of deep peace and joy. In that place near God, you will begin to learn a little about him. You will learn, perhaps, what unconditional love is. You will begin to realise that you can climb up onto that rock near him no matter what sort of state you are in, and his welcoming embrace will be as strong as ever. You will realise what it truly means to be loved. Certain gospel stories – the story of the Prodigal Son, for example – will have a new and deeper meaning for you, as you begin to experience for yourself the truth that they illustrate. This is a happy time, the period of your prayer flies by, and you seem to have little or no distractions. You are drawn to prayer for the joy and the peace it gives you. It is a time for resting from the exertions you experienced in undertaking the climb in the first place.

Life experiences

You will find that your daily life too will be influenced by this new-found peace and happiness. The world will begin to look different. It is a little bit like falling in love. When I first began to pray in this way, I was living in Luxembourg, and I remember how, as I walked to work in the mornings along the Rue de Beggen, where I lived, the colours of the sky and the trees seemed more vivid, and I felt enclosed in a little cocoon of happiness that I was sure must be visible.

You will also find that situations and problems that previously caused you difficulty will now be easier to deal with. This is, in the main, because your own attitude towards them is changing. You are gaining a new perspective on life's events and are beginning to view them from the perspective of eternity.

It is not uncommon during this period for people to overcome personal problems that had beset them for years. An addiction may suddenly become a thing of the past. A person whose very appearance on the horizon had previously caused your hackles to rise may now stand revealed as someone in pain, someone you find it in yourself now to welcome. This is a happy time, a sort of honeymoon period. You feel benevolent towards all humanity. You may feel that this is what prayer and the spiritual life are all about. Life is good: prayer has made sense of everything.

You may therefore wonder what it is that has gone wrong when things begin to change.

The cleft of the rock
For change they most certainly will, as you move into the second stage of prayer. Just as my niece Laila had eventually to be weaned away from milk and introduced to the solid food she needed in order to grow and develop, so will you have to be weaned away from the pleasures of the early days of prayer in order to be fed with the solid food that your deepest self needs to grow and develop. There is a danger lurking in the prayer you have been enjoying until now. The danger is that you might become more attracted to the pleasures of prayer than to God, who is your sole reason for being there. Or, as the old spiritual masters used to put it, you may become drawn more to the consolations of God than to the God of consolations.

And 'So what?' you might ask. Is God like a jealous partner, who wants all attention for himself? Yes, God wants all your attention for himself, but not from jealousy. Remember what we said earlier was God's sole wish for us: to bring us to the fullness of life and freedom. All the work that God undertakes in your regard is aimed at that end. Your freedom is inseparable from the fullness of life that God desires for you. In other words, as long as you are not free, you will not be able to enjoy the fullness of life. If you look back now from this point in your spiritual life, you will see that many of the old chains that kept you captive have begun to weaken and break as a result of your practice of prayer. The attraction you feel for prayer and for spiritual things is greater than the attraction you previously felt for things that were not good for you. But there is a subtle danger here, and that is that you might just exchange one sort of imprisonment for another. You might now become 'addicted' to prayer, and in that addiction, you will be every bit as unfree as you were before.

A simple test will show you whether you are free in your practice of prayer or not at this point in your development. Imagine the following scenario. You have set aside thirty minutes every evening for prayer. You really look forward to this time, which is for you a winding-down, relaxing time, but above all, it is a time when you feel you are at home in the truest and deepest sense. It is a time when you draw strength from God for whatever the next day may bring, a time when his unconditional love reassures you and calms your regrets over mistakes made during the day. And then, this evening, just as you are about to start your thirty minutes, your neighbour knocks at the door. She badly needs you to look after her children for the next two hours, as she has to leave in a hurry to deal with a family crisis. This puts paid to any hope of having your prayer time tonight.

How do you feel? More likely than not, you feel a mixture of annoyance, frustration and disappointment at having to give up your prayer. If that is so, you are not free. If you were truly free, you would feel just as happy to look after your neighbour's children as you would to spend thirty minutes in prayer, because you would know that God gives himself to you in whatever the present moment holds.

Because you are still unfree, God needs to take over your prayer. Up to this it was natural. The emotions you experienced were all natural emotions of joy, peace, love, and so on. But now, your prayer must become mystical.

48

Experience during prayer

The words 'mystic' and 'mystical' scare the life out of some people. This is probably because they misunderstand the term 'mysticism', which they confuse with the extraordinary and the paranormal. A mystical life may, and sometimes does involve supernatural visitations and paranormal experiences, but they are not essential, and when they occur, they tend, as I said earlier, to be an overflow into the senses of what is occurring all the time in all of us at the deep level where God dwells. We all have a capacity for mysticism, because we all have within us a spark of the divine. When you begin to get in touch with that spark of God within you, when you embark on a relationship with him, you begin to live a mystical life. Prayer can be said to become mystical when God takes over the principal role.

What will the experience of God taking over be like for you? One thing is sure: at first, it won't feel like God is doing anything at all. In fact, it is much more likely to feel like you have somehow or other gone backwards. Moses must have felt a bit like that when God placed him in the cleft of that rock. Gone was the bright sunlight, the panoramic view, the spaciousness, the feelings of love, joy and peace. Instead, there was poor Moses, cramped up inside a dark, damp and clammy space. He probably felt a little chilly. The daylight would only have been visible through a crack. Moses was no longer in charge as he had been when he climbed up and stood upon the rock. God had taken over, and it didn't feel comfortable.

So too for you, when God begins to take over your prayer, it will not feel comfortable. The first thing you will probably become aware of is that it is no longer easy. If you have been using scripture meditation as your focusing exercise, you will begin to find a great difficulty in doing it now. You will find it impossible to picture a scene, and you will end up tired and frustrated. If your exercise has been following the breath, or the use of a sacred word or other mantra, then far from it leading you into stillness, you will find yourself becoming obsessed with your breathing or with the mantra. Most of your prayer time will be taken up with trying to get your meditation, breathing or mantra right.

If you notice something like this happening to your prayer, you will need first to rule out any natural cause. The same effects can be produced by over-tiredness, illness or extreme anxiety. They can also be produced when you are living a lifestyle that is out of synch with the practice of prayer: so, for example, a lifestyle that is promiscuous, gluttonous, or careless of the good of others cannot co-exist with a life of prayer. Either your lifestyle will stifle your prayer, or your prayer will gradually change your lifestyle. The effects can also be produced by simple negligence about your prayer life: not sticking as much as possible to your regular prayer time, only praying now and then. In those circumstances, your prayer life will weaken and die.

How can you know if it is one of the above, rather than God taking over, that is the cause of your seeming inability to pray? This question is one that people frequently agonise over at this stage. The answer to it is complicated by the fact that God may well be taking over even in circumstances where you are over-tired, stressed or ill – and in fact, he not infrequently is. But there is one unfailing test: if your seeming inability to pray is due principally to God taking over, then you will be conscious of an anxiety about your prayer. The very fact that you are querying what is happening is an indication of that anxiety. You will probably find yourself consulting books or people you think might be able to help you. You will be fearful of having lost something somehow through your own fault, yet without being able to point to any instance where you might have been at fault.

This is a time in your spiritual life when it would be wise to consult an experienced person, if you are not already doing so. You will find more about spiritual direction and its role in your life in chapter 9. A spiritual director or other experienced person will help you to discern whether God is indeed taking over, or whether the cause of your difficulty is one of the other things I've mentioned above. Your director will also give you the re-assurance you need that this is a good development, and this reassurance is sorely needed. Indeed, another sign that God is taking over is the joy that most people feel upon getting this reassurance. It seems to confirm something that in their deepest centre they already knew, although their anxious, conscious mind just could not accept it.

So, if your prayer has become difficult after a long period of peace and joy and attraction to prayer, if your usual method has become difficult to adhere to, and now you find yourself surreptitiously looking at the clock and wondering how thirty minutes could seem so long, if at the same time you feel a nagging anxiety that you must be doing something wrong, and if you have been reassured by your director or other wise person then rejoice! You are not doing anything wrong – in fact, you are not doing anything at all. God has taken you and put you in the cleft of the rock in a place near him. God has taken over your prayer.

Praying in the cleft of the rock
So, you have been reassured that God is taking over your prayer. What should you now do when you go to prayer? Have you any role at all? It is important first of all to bear in mind that the various methods we have looked at for quietening ourselves and disposing ourselves for prayer are nothing more than that: methods. The meditation on the gospel scene, the following of the breath, the use of the sacred word – these things are not themselves the aim of the exercise, but just the means to an end.

What is that end? The end is to be able to be present to God, who is always present to you. Now that God is himself bringing you into his presence, there is no need for you to use any method to get there. Those methods will no longer be of any use, which is why you have been finding them impossible to put into practice.

So abandon them! Yes, this will probably seem rather alarming at first, a little bit like the first time your father removed the stabilisers on your bicycle and you found that you were balancing precariously on two wheels. But just as your father had realised before you did that you had already found your balance, so God knows that you no longer need the stabilisers of method and good feelings to keep you at prayer.

Your prayer now is time given to God. You are there now for him, not for yourself. Your prayer will take the form of simply waiting, not doing anything, wasting time, putting it beyond any use to yourself. This will feel very strange at first, but it might help if you thought of it as time spent listening. When you are totally present to him in deep contemplative prayer, God speaks directly to you, teaching you secretly about himself, making himself known to you in a mysterious way that you cannot understand.

If you find the idea of listening unhelpful, then you might like to consider another definition of this kind of prayer: standing unprotected before God. This, as we saw earlier, is the way Sister Wendy Beckett describes prayer in her book *Sister Wendy on Prayer*. Think of what it means if you stand unprotected before someone. You are without defences, so you cannot offer resistance to anything that happens. The corollary of that is that you accept everything. This is the start of a deep surrender to God, a surrender that will end by bringing you into total freedom and the fullness of life.

So all you are required to do at this stage in your development is to be there. This is the time for turning up faithfully every day for your prayer time, even if at first it seems a total waste. What is essential on your side is to stay where God in his love has placed you, so that he can accomplish his work. So a good idea during this period would be to begin your prayer with an act of trust: 'Lord, I know you love me. You know me through and through. You know that all I want during this period is to be near you. It doesn't feel as if I'm near you, but I believe that I am, and I trust you that you are beside me and that you will keep me safe.'

The dreaming butterfly

For many people, the reassurance that it is alright to let go of methods and practices results in an extraordinary feeling of liberation. It's as though they have been given permission to go through a door that they only now realise has been there in front of them. If this is your experience, thank God for it! It is a wonderfully joyful thing. A new deep attraction for prayer makes itself felt, and whereas before, prayer time was drudgery, now it is a wonderful experience of letting go. Such people would be hard put to it to explain why prayer is now so attractive. There is not much in the way of content, or of anything happening, that they can point to. But what they can say is that they would not miss their prayer time for the entire world.

But it's also not uncommon for other people to feel slightly panicked by the expanse of what seems like empty time stretching ahead of them. If this happens to you, don't run away; face into it. The experience of emptiness is a good one. We are afraid of emptiness because we do not recognise it as a friend. Emptiness means the absence of form and content. We are comfortable with form and content because they are things that can be perceived by our senses. Emptiness cannot be perceived in itself. We only know it is there by the absence of things that we can perceive.

But God is neither form nor content. God is no-thing. God is pure spirit, which to your senses will seem like nothing. Up to this, God has been giving himself to you in prayer through your senses, through your pleasant, peaceful and fulfilling experiences. But nothing that your senses perceive or your mind imagines can give you any real idea of what God is. At this stage in prayer, God wants to give himself directly to your spirit, your deepest self, the part of you that is at home with God's spirit. So here is a paradox (one of the many in the spiritual life): God is closer to you now that he was in that earlier, more pleasurable form of prayer, but that greater closeness feels like its opposite, absence. The poet, Paul Murray, describes it in this way:

But what a weight of absence
O Nameless One!
as you leaned against me
suddenly

> like a wall of air,
> as you gazed into my eyes
> and stared through me,
> your eyes and your gaze incurious
> yet all-perceiving,
> your dark eyes
> like the closed wings
> of a dreaming butterfly.[20]

Reassure yourself with this thought: your deepest self is at home with what seems like emptiness to you now, and as your deepest self becomes progressively more free, you will find that the whole of you will share in this ease and at-home-ness. Remember what we said at the beginning of this book: there are two people involved in every prayer encounter: you and God. And God is always active during prayer, always giving more and more of himself to you.

A helpful way both to remind yourself that God is present in spite of a feeling of absence and to ground yourself in the truth, is to start your prayer by telling God in all honesty how you feel. If you feel panicked, say so. If you feel bored, or if you feel you would rather be anywhere else but where you are right now, say that. You will find that in some strange way and at some deep level, a connection has been established that will enable you to rest more peacefully where you are for a little while. When agitation arises again, tell God about it, and once more, this will bring you back to the truth and the reality of the present and what is taking place there.

If you are grounded in the truth, you are grounded in God. Remember that Jesus said, 'I am the Way, the Truth and the Life'.[21] And he also said 'The truth will make you free.'[22]

Life experiences
Life experiences during this time vary. For some people, this development in their prayer coincides with an external life change that allows them to devote more time to prayer than before. If this happen to you, then the experience is likely to be profound

and deeply satisfying, as you will have the opportunity to become accustomed to the new way of praying in a shorter space of time. Very soon, you will become aware of the subtle attraction that invariably develops once you get used to this new path. Prayer will become a place that you look forward to with a passion. You will find yourself full of gratitude to God.

But whether or not there is a change in your external circumstances, you will probably find a rather strange thing happening externally. Faults and failings that, up to this, you had managed to conceal very well (not least from yourself) now take on a new vigour and strength, and make themselves clearly known, not just to you (you could cope with that!) but, horror of horrors, often to other people as well. What is happening? Well, at this stage, God is freeing you at a deeper level than before. undoing chains that have imprisoned and crippled you for a long time. Chains that had been forged in babyhood and even earlier, during your time in your mother's womb, are now being cleaned of rust, oiled, and opened. But God does not do this without your co-operation and full consent. It is therefore necessary for you to become fully aware of the places in you which need to be liberated. And sometimes, in order for us to truly accept our weaknesses, they have to be manifested to others as well as to ourselves. We are all very good at denial, but it's very difficult to deny the existence of a fault that other people can see!

This can be a deeply shocking experience at first. It will seem to you that, far from getting closer to God, you are moving away, and that in fact, you are in a worse state morally than you have ever been in your life. But something else is also happening. Awful as the revelation of your real self may be, it will not take you away from prayer. The secret wisdom that you are gaining in the cleft of the rock is guiding your deepest self very strongly during this period.

During this time, you will, in spite of everything be aware in some deep core of yourself that all is well. Your inner light will guide you infallibly along the path of an ever-deepening trust in God, on whom, as you now begin to see clearly, you totally depend for everything that you need. When this period has passed, you will realise a great truth: no-one is good save God alone. Your virtues (and believe it or not, there will come a day when you will be able to see them and indeed, celebrate them) are only yours because they have been given to you as a gift.

St John of the Cross has a metaphor for this stage in your spiritual life which I have always loved. It is the metaphor of fire working on a log of wood. Here is what he says, in his rather amusing (to our ears) sixteenth-century way:

> ... for material fire, acting upon wood, first of all begins to dry it, by driving out its moisture and causing it to shed the water which it contained within itself. Then it makes it black, dark and unsightly, and even to give forth a bad odour ... as it dries it little by little, it brings out and drives away all the dark and unsightly accidents which are contrary to the nature of fire. And, finally, it begins to kindle it externally and give it heat, and at last transforms it into itself and makes it as beautiful as fire.

Quaint as this description may be, it is stunningly accurate. The fire of which St John of the Cross speaks is of course God, or God's love (which are one and the same thing). When he says the fire makes the wood 'black, dark and unsightly, and even to give forth a bad odour', this is exactly what happens.

A story of old beds

During a period I spent living in a contemplative community in France, I had a striking experience of this. There is probably nothing quite like living in close contact with a small group of other people in a confined situation to bring out someone's true character, a fact of which the producers of Channel Four's *Big Brother* and other similar reality shows are well aware. When I joined this community, my idea of myself was of a mature, self-possessed woman, capable of maintaining her *sang-froid* in most situations. Instead, after some months had passed, the nuns began to see a very unpleasant side of me. I openly resented being corrected, and the novice mistress told me that I often appeared arrogant and that the younger nuns were often intimidated by my attitude. In case you might think that I am exaggerating a bit, let me give you a concrete example – and bear in mind that this was just one occurrence out of many!

One Sunday afternoon, I was about to leave the house set off for a walk in the woods that surrounded the monastery, when I was surprised to hear voices and laughter coming from a nearby staircase. This was unusual, as silence was the general rule in the house, so my curiosity was aroused. I waited, craning my neck to look up the stairs. For a few moments, nothing was visible, but more muffled laughter and intriguing bumps came from higher up, around the bend of the staircase. Then the novice-mistress appeared, descending backwards, arms spread wide. She was followed by my fellow novice and one of the younger nuns struggling with one end of a small iron bedstead, which appeared to be pushing them down the staircase. The other end was held by two more nuns who were clearly having some difficulty controlling matters. Everybody seemed to be having a lot of fun.

They didn't see me. I stood there in the shelter of a doorway and watched the proceedings. All the younger members of the community were there. I was the only one who had been left out. A dark mist filled my brain. I wanted to yell and scream at them. I wanted to lie on the floor like a small child and throw a tantrum. Using all my will-power, I forced myself to turn away and walk through the glass door into the garden. Outside, I stood still. Everything in me wanted to go back to let them know that I knew they had left me out. I knew I was being ridiculous. I tried to pray. It seemed to me that I had reached a decisive moment: if I was serious about the life I was trying to live, I would now walk down to the woods, hand over the hurt to God and get on with things. I took a few steps towards the woods, then turned round and went back. The hallway was deserted, but voices from above, together with the iron bedstead and other bric-a-brac in the hall bore witness to the ongoing work. I started to climb the stairs. There they were, all of them, around the first bend, struggling with another bed, laughing and enjoying themselves together.

'Can I help?' I asked loudly.

Five startled faces turned towards me.

'No, we're fine, thanks', said the novice mistress, smiling at first, but then, seeing my thunderous expression, and realising that this was something more than a polite offer, she came down towards me anxiously, ushering me back towards the hall.

'What on earth is this about?' she asked quietly.

'I simply want to know if I can help, that's all.'

'We were just bringing down some old beds from the attic, but everything is almost done now. But thanks anyway. Were you off for a walk?'

I stared at her. I was now beyond all reasoning.

'It doesn't look to me as if you've finished', I said, and brushing past her rudely I mounted the stairs and accosted the nun who was at the receiving end of the second iron bed.

'I'll take that!' I said, almost thrusting her aside.

Astonished, she let go and moved out of my way. I was conscious of five pairs of eyes upon me. All the laughter stopped. Down we went, me clinging grimly to my corner of the bed. We reached the hall in total silence and set down the bed. Everyone stood there uneasily. My fury increased. So they only enjoyed themselves when I wasn't there!

'Is there any more?' I demanded.

The unfortunate novice-mistress found her voice.

'No,' she said. 'There isn't any more. Thanks for your help.'

Marching past her, I made my way back to the door and went outside. I stood there, dazed. What had I just done? My head was still spinning and my heart was racing. My anger had not died down, but added to it now was a sense of total humiliation. I had made a complete fool of myself.

If by now you are laughing, I don't blame you. In retrospect, the story is an amusing one, but it clearly illustrates what we have just been talking about. At this stage of your prayer life, faults and flaws that have been carefully hidden under a mask of respectability and acceptable behaviour refuse to be hidden any longer. They emerge into the full light of day so that you cannot but acknowledge their existence. In my own case, I had been vaguely aware even at the time that I no longer seemed able to keep up the sort of appearances that one kept up in the world; it was as though my defences had been swept away and I was appearing as I really was. St John of the Cross was quite right.

Why is this good? There are two reasons that I can think of. First, by bringing your hidden flaws into your own awareness, God ensures your co-operation with him in the liberation of your deepest self. Second, by making them visible to others, God prevents us from deluding ourselves that we are able to over-come them alone. The experience of our inability to keep up ap-pearances brings us face to face with the truth of our own weak-ness and total dependence upon God. This is what it means to be humble.

A new freedom

But if I have given you the impression that this is a dark and dif-ficult stage, let me now correct that impression and say that in-deed it is not. Going back to our analogy of the cleft in the rock, there is, after all, daylight visible from there, the sun can shine in and you will often feel its warmth. Indeed, the warmth and the light that you will experience at these times will be stronger than any experience of your earlier days, because now the warmth and light is penetrating deeper. Blockages inside you which have been there for years are shifting, and the light is reaching places that previously were very dark.

During this time, you will begin to notice that old hardened attitudes are weakening, that you are becoming more flexible. At times, the cleft of the rock expands in such a way that you will feel like someone who has come out of a cramped dark place into warm sunlight and fragrant air. You begin to stretch and flex inner muscles that you didn't know you had, revelling in a new sense of well-being. You are coming very close to discovering what true happiness is. And what is different – and wonderful – about your new joy and peace is this: it is not dependent on external circumstances.

I will place my hand over you

The third stage of prayer begins almost imperceptibly. During the period in which your spiritual and prayer life is 'growing up', so to speak, God, as we saw, begins to take over your prayer, and to lead you deeper. The deeper your prayer becomes, the less perceptible it will be to your senses. Your prayer is always moving into a greater simplicity, until ultimately a point will come where there is simply no separation between prayer and the rest of your life. Your spiritual life will then have reached maturity. That moment comes when your entire being, and not just your deepest self, is united with God. But before that moment can arrive, the work – God's work – that was begun during the second stage of prayer has to go deeper, right to your deepest centre, so as to complete the liberation of your deepest self.

Experience during prayer

What will this feel like to you while it is happening? Think again of Moses. What happened to him while he was in the cleft of the rock? God placed his hand over him so that he would be protected while the glory of God passed by him.

What does this mean? God's glory is the essence of himself: his life and his love. It is nothing less than the relationship of love that exists within the Blessed Trinity. We might even call it God's own prayer – the Father communing with the Son in the unity of the Holy Spirit. If this sounds more or less incomprehensible, don't be alarmed. It is incomprehensible – our finite sense literally cannot take it in. But what it means is that at this point, you will not really be praying at all: instead, you will be drawn into the prayer of God within you. This is what God shares with you in deep contemplative prayer. In this sort of prayer, you come to know God in a way that goes beyond anything you could learn about him from books or from the teaching of others. God's glory passes beside you.

But because you are human and not a total spirit, because you are still living on this earth, this experience would be too much for your human nature to bear. You need God's protection for it. God, therefore, will place his hand over you. When God placed his hand over Moses, Moses, I imagine, was unable to see anything. Daylight was completely blotted out while God's glory was passing by. So too, in the early part of this stage of prayer, you will see nothing – you will experience God's protecting hand covering you as darkness. Francis Thompson has words for this:

> Is my gloom, after all,
> shade of his hand, outstretched caressingly?[23]

It is in this secret darkness that God's glory passes right beside you, communicating itself to you and filling you with its secret wisdom. All you need to do is to be there, and to trust. There is nothing to be afraid of, because you are held safely in the shelter of the Most High. Even if your earlier peace and joy disappear, even if you are assailed by inner noise and distractions, don't be afraid. The noise and distractions are at a superficial level only; in the depths of your being wonderful things are happening. So your behaviour during prayer must be the same as in the previous stage: just be faithful, be patient, stand before God unprotected and in utter truthfulness, and wait.

At this stage in prayer, if there are any vestiges of structure left, any input from yourself, you may find you have to abandon them, just as you had to abandon the various methods at the time when you were praying in the cleft of the rock. What is essential is that you should not attempt to control the prayer in any way. Think about it: it is the prayer of God: how can you possibly control it? Any attempt to put shape or structure on prayer at this stage will result in great frustration for you.

A friend of mine called Betty became terribly worried because she thought she had, as she put it herself, lost the ability to pray. Trying to explain what was happening, she said that it was as if a door that she used to go through without even noticing it had vanished, and now she was faced with a wall that she couldn't penetrate. Betty had been praying for many years, and had experienced good times and difficult times, but no matter how hard it had been, she always came away from prayer knowing that she had prayed. Now she came away feeling that she had spent the entire time trying to pray, without any success. What was happening?

A friend to whom she took this problem listened carefully. He saw that Betty was very upset. This in itself was an indication to him that her inability to pray probably didn't stem from carelessness or a falling-away in her spiritual life. He asked her to describe what she did every day when her prayer time arrived.

'Well,' she said, I light my candle and sit down, and then I say a prayer to the Holy Spirit in order to begin the prayer.'

'And then?' her friend invited.

'Then I begin to feel acutely anxious because I don't know what to do next,' Betty said. 'And the rest of the time passes with my making huge, useless efforts to get over or through that wall! I used to get great joy from the idea that I was standing unprotected before God. The very thought of that seemed to bring me to a deep place – I didn't have to do any more than recall where I was. But now ...'

Her friend was silent for a moment or two. Then he said,

'Betty, it sounds to me as if you are trying to pray.'

'Well, yes!' she said, sounding a bit exasperated. 'Of course I'm trying to pray! That's what I've been telling you for the past fifteen minutes!'

'Then here's my advice', said her friend. 'Stop trying. The next time your prayer period comes around, don't begin with the prayer to the Holy Spirit. Just sit down.'

Betty looked doubtful.

'And then what?' she asked.

'Then nothing', her friend said. 'There is no need for you to do anything, because God is doing everything. His prayer is going on within you, and all you have to do is be there. Sometimes, he may let you be aware of it, other times not. But no matter whether you are aware or not, you will be radiated upon.'

Betty took her friend's advice. The next time she went to prayer, she did not begin with her usual prayer to the Holy Spirit. It felt strange but she persevered. She sat down, and made no other effort at all. When the hour was up, she realised that for the first time in months, she hadn't felt anxious or frustrated during prayer. As the days went on, she realised that not only was there an absence of anxiety, but there was an increasing, although very subtle, sense of something else.

'It's a feeling of rightness', she said, reporting back to her friend. 'A feeling that I'm in the right place. And', she added, sounding slightly astonished, 'it's so restful!'

Betty was correct. This is what Jesus promised when he said 'Come to me all you who labour, and I will give you rest.' It is in this prayer that we really begin to understand that his yoke is easy, and his burden light.

Life experiences

Arrival at this point in prayer often coincides with some painful life-experience. This can take many forms: it may be the death or illness of a loved one, it may be your own illness, or the loss of a job, or the break-up of a relationship. Or it may be a hurtful misunderstanding. Whatever it is, if it happens to you remember that you are in the hands of one who loves you. There is a purpose to what is happening, and that purpose is to help you to learn to trust.

Trust is probably the most difficult lesson we have to learn in the course of the spiritual life. We pay lip service to it: we say we trust God, but when the chips are down, we really don't. If we did, we would never try to avoid painful experiences in the way that we do, because we would know that somehow, in a way beyond our understanding, they were merely vehicles to bring us into greater freedom and a greater fullness of life.

In my own case, it happened in this way. Some time after the episode of the old beds that I related above, the community with which I had hoped to live decided (rightly!) that I was not cut out for their way of life. They asked me to leave, a move which left me totally devastated. There I was, without home or employment, feeling that I had lost the whole purpose of my life. But worst of all, my prayer, which throughout that year and a half had comforted me and given me the strength to keep going, had now all but vanished. All I found when I tried to pray was a whirling mind and churning emotions of anger and bitterness.

After several months of this anguish, a fortuitous encounter with a spiritual director led me first to stop trying to pray in the old way, and instead to just be there, present to God. Little by little, things began to change. Prayer began to give me strength in a new hidden way. And then an amazing thing happened: I began to see a meaning and a purpose in the whole awful thing. I slowly began to see that the experience of losing everything had been absolutely essential to my spiritual journey – so essential, in fact, that I now realised it was the sole reason why I had been led to join the community in the first place. In other words, leaving was the whole point of going there. From that point, my life changed. The more I lived out of the truth of that experience, the more I realised that it is absolutely essential that a moment should come in the spiritual quest where all your resources, all your plans and hopes and dreams, are taken away. That is a moment of crisis. You can then do one of two things: abandon the quest as being hopeless, or turn to God in the most absolute way, and allow him to 'be God'. If you take that second option, God is at last free to act in your life as he wants, and your life will become directed along his path. Such a realisation is a huge breakthrough, and it can only happen in a moment of deep pain.

But there will also be very positive life experiences at this time. The fruit of all of God's secret activity will become obvious to you little by little outside of the time of prayer. You will become at the same time more aware of secret weaknesses and less anxious about them, although feeling a deep sorrow for your failure to respond to God's love. You will also notice a greater sensitivity in your dealings with other people, and increased understanding and compassion for their weaknesses. The scriptures will speak to you in new ways – and indeed this is a time to read scripture often outside of prayer time, because it will be illuminated by the secret wisdom you have acquired during prayer. What is happening? During prayer, God keeps you covered with his hand while he shares so much of himself with you; at the end of prayer, he lifts his hand and allows you to see his back, as he did with Moses.

So there is no need to be afraid when these changes take place in your prayer. They are good: something wonderful is taking place. Please don't resist; instead, increase your faith and your trust. This is the time to remember and pray the words of Psalm 90:

You who live in the shelter of the Most High,
Who abide in the shadow of the Almighty,
Will say to the Lord, 'My refuge and my fortress,
My God, in whom I trust.'
Because you have made the Lord your refuge,
The Most High your dwelling-place,
No evil shall befall you,
No scourge come near your tent.
Those who love me, I will deliver;
I will protect those who know my name,
When they call me, I will answer them;
I will be with them in trouble.
I will rescue them and honour them.
With long life I will satisfy them,
And show them my salvation.

CHAPTER FIVE

Dealing with Difficulties in Prayer

Distractions

Distractions are a perennial problem during prayer. What is a distraction? A distraction is anything that pulls you away from your presence to God and God's presence to you. Distractions can be external – people or events that take you away, someone calling at the door, the phone ringing – or internal: memories that draw you into the past or imaginings that pull you into the future. Everyone has experienced them, but it is not always easy to distinguish a distraction from something that is not one.

Vincent, a friend of mine, has told me that he was so tormented by the constant passage of thoughts through his mind during prayer that he was on the point of giving the whole thing up. Fortunately, he decided first to discuss this with his spiritual director.

'I'm just not cut out for it', he said glumly.

'Nonsense,' his director said briskly. 'The person who is not cut out for prayer hasn't yet been born! Your spirit needs prayer in the same way as your body needs food. You wouldn't say you weren't cut out to eat, would you?'

Vincent wasn't convinced.

'But I just can't get rid of all these thoughts,' he protested. 'They make it impossible for me to pray.'

'Well, of course you can't get rid of thoughts,' his director said. 'If you had no thoughts, you'd be dead! Your mind has to think; that's what it's for. But thoughts are not distractions; that's where you are making your mistake. Imagine a friend comes to visit you one day when your wife has gone out and left you looking after the children. You are delighted to see this friend, you haven't seen him for years and you have a lot of catching up to do. You send the kids off upstairs to their play-room, from which, after a bit, comes the most appalling racket. They seem to be playing football up there. 'Excuse me a minute,' you say to your friend, and you run upstairs and bawl the kids out. You come back down. 'Now where were we?' you say to your friend. You manage to pick up the threads of the conversa-tion. After another few minutes, more bedlam breaks out above. You excuse yourself again, and setting your teeth, you climb the stairs and restore order. This time, when you return to your friend, you have one ear cocked for sounds from above. You can't really concentrate on the conversation any more, and after a bit your friend says, 'Look, Vincent, I can see I've called at a bad time. You've your hands full here. Let's leave it to another day.'

'Does this sound familiar?' his director asked Vincent, 'Is this how you deal with your thoughts?'

'Well, yes,' Vincent admitted, laughing. 'But what else can I do? I can't just ignore them.'

'Can't you?' said his director. 'Let's look at an alternative scenario to the one above. The friend comes, you send the kids upstairs, all hell breaks loose as per before. However, you ignore it. You are so anxious to talk to your friend that you concentrate on that. Little by little, the sounds from upstairs become back-ground noises. You notice them, you are aware of them (indeed, if total silence fell, then you would be worried!) but you don't engage with them.'

Many of us, like Vincent, mistake thoughts for distractions. They are not, they are just thoughts. What, then, is a distraction? A distraction is anything that pulls you out of the truth and into falsehood – in other words, anything that removes you from the truth that is the present moment. So, for example, although someone calling to the door or ringing you on the phone may physically take you away from prayer, that may not be a distrac-tion. It might be a very necessary matter that you should attend to. On the other hand, if someone called to the door and said 'I'm just on my way to the cinema, will you come?' and you dropped everything and went, that would be a distraction! As an aside, can I just say here that if you can, it's a good idea to turn off your phone during the time you have allocated to prayer – unless, of course, you are expecting a call that it would be irresponsible to ignore.

Internal events
What about thoughts? Well, thoughts become distractions when you engage with them. You engage with them in two different ways. One way is like the father in the imaginary scenario above – you become obsessed with trying to get rid of them, to the point where you are no longer able to concentrate on why you are there and the One you are with. The other way is by letting them draw you in.

So, for example, while I am praying, I might suddenly re-member an unpleasant encounter I had with a colleague the day before. I hadn't acquitted myself too well. This memory is just a thought, it is not a distraction. Not yet anyway. But if the memo-ry prompts me to think what I might have said, and I begin to reflect on that, then within seconds I have embarked upon a whole imaginary scenario of how the encounter might have developed if I had said this or that.

Or the thought of a forthcoming evening out with friends, an event I am looking forward to, flashes upon my mind. It is just a thought, no more than that. But if I begin to linger on the thought with anticipation, then before I know it, I am planning what I will wear, or what restaurant we will go to, and I am in a full-blown distraction.

How can I avoid this? Vincent's director had the right advice: notice the thought and let it go. So when the thought of the un-pleasant encounter with the colleague comes into my mind, I can simply say to myself, oh, there's a thought, that's all it is. So I have noticed it. Now I can gently let it go. It will swim past along the stream of my consciousness, and it will be followed by others. I can treat them in the same way, notice them, let them go. If I find I am becoming obsessed with them, or they are drawing me in seductively, I can just turn back to whatever my initial method for calming my mind was – gospel scene, following the breath, sacred word – until the thought has floated by, out of sight.

The important thing to realise is that thoughts will continually come and go: they are not distractions unless and until you engage with them. Sometimes you have engaged with them almost before you realise it, and you wake up to the realisation that you have been a million miles away for quite a while. Never mind: you can turn then once again to your gospel scene, your breathing, your sacred word, until you are once more back in the present. This is not some endurance test or striving for the perfect prayer period; it is a meeting with a Lover, and no matter how far you may wander away during the period, he will always be there when you come back.

As long as you are focused on getting rid of thoughts, you are not fully in the present moment. As long as you are drawn in to memories of the past or thoughts of the future, you are not fully in the present moment. You are distracted from the only truth.

What do I mean when I say that the present moment is the only truth? An example might help. I've already mentioned Anna. Well, some years ago, she was diagnosed with cancer. The day her doctor told her the news was a dreadful day for Anna, her husband Kieran and their twelve year old daughter Rachel. The doctor explained that the tumour, although a large one, was operable, and that if he succeeded in removing it all, the prognosis was good. However, there was a danger that the cancer had spread, and further tests were necessary. Although these would be done with all speed, they would not know the results for a further ten days.

The first few days of that period were the worst Anna had ever spent. Various scenarios, each one worse than the last, played themselves over and over in her head. She saw herself walking with Kieran into the doctor's rooms and being told that she had only a month to live. She imagined Rachel's devastation at the loss of her mother, and couldn't bear it. Or she saw herself ill during months of chemotherapy, unable to work, and wondered how they would continue to keep up their mortgage payments. She could neither eat nor sleep, and began to look really ill.

Anna had, for some time before this, been living a consciously spiritual life, and had set aside thirty minutes of every day in her busy life to pray and meditate. Now she found she could no longer pray, tormented as she was by fearful thoughts. On the fifth day, she rang Rita, her spiritual mentor, a woman who had been giving her regular guidance in her spiritual journey. Rita listened in silence to Anna's distraught and almost incoherent explanation of what was happening. When she drew to a close, she asked her: 'What is upsetting you so much?' Thinking Rita hadn't heard a word she said, Anna began the story all over again. Rita stopped her. 'I heard everything you told me', she said, 'but I want you to think about what exactly it is that is upsetting you, right now, at this very moment.' Anna was silent for a minute. Then she said, 'I'm upset because of what might happen.'

'Tell me what is happening right at this moment,' said Rita. 'Where are you? What are you doing?'

'I'm sitting here at home speaking to you on the phone,' said Anna, puzzled.

'Exactly.' Rita said. 'At the moment, right now, you have not left your daughter. You are not in the middle of chemotherapy. You feel well, and if you had not been told you had cancer, you would be happily living your life. But your life is now! This moment is the only certain and true thing about your life. The future doesn't exist, so it is not the truth. It is something unreal, untrue, non-existent, which has made you so upset. There is nothing even remotely upsetting about this actual moment in your life, where you are having a telephone conversation and waiting for your daughter to come home from school. So, when you go to prayer, just recall that the only truth is that you are there, alive and praying, and see how that works for you.'

Anna put this into practice. It wasn't easy the first or the second time, but by the third time, she had begun to get the hang of it. It was all about living in the present moment, she realised. If you don't fully live in the present moment, then your life is passing you by unnoticed. Anna found a new serenity beginning to grow, a serenity which increased as time went on and which carried her through the difficult stages of her illness. Now that she is fully restored to health again, she realises that she has learned an invaluable lesson – not just for times of prayer, but for every stage in her life.

External events

In all of this, I am, of course, speaking of distractions that come from within. External distractions are another matter. To a certain extent, these are much more within your control, as I've already said. You can, for example, turn the phone off during your prayer period, both land line and mobile. (Yes, really! You won't die without it for one hour or less!) You can ignore the doorbell if you are not expecting anyone, and you can ask the members of your household to respect your privacy for a short period. However, there are other external distractions that you cannot control – the workmen who choose that moment to begin drilling in the roadway outside your house, the loud rock music coming from next door – but these won't happen every time, and when they do, you will just have to grit your teeth and bear it. There is a way, too, in which you can turn things like that into prayer – not a very peaceful prayer, it is true, but in the end, you are there for God, not for yourself.

Carmelite nuns have their prayer period all gathered together in their chapel. St Thérèse of Lisieux tells us in her autobiography that when she was a young nun, another member of the community whose place in the chapel was right behind Thérèse had a most annoying habit of regularly clicking her teeth (loose dentures, perhaps?) during prayer. This almost drove Thérèse out of her mind, until she hit upon the idea of listening for it and offering it to God as some beautiful music.

While that might be a rather extreme way of dealing with the problem, what you could instead do is pray for the workmen drilling the road; for their lives and personal problems and worries. You could pray for the health and happiness of the young teenagers next door and for their protection from harm as they go through life.

In short, don't get hung up on distractions. You can be sure of one thing: something is always happening interiorly during prayer, no matter what distractions are active on the surface. Something of great moment is going on at a level too deep to grasp. Just sit there as quietly as you are able, looking at your icon, if you find that helpful, or closing your eyes if that is better for you.

Persistent thoughts

However, from time to time, a seeming distraction may be something entirely different. If you find one particular thought returning persistently no matter how often you go back to your breathing or your sacred word – particularly if this occurs during several prayer periods – then it may be worth examining it more closely to see whether in fact this is something that is rising up in your prayer so that you might bring it before God.

Another friend of mine, Denis, experienced this. It happened during a time when his home life had become very difficult. His wife had developed Alzheimer's, which made her behaviour irrational and unpredictable. During his prayer one day, Denis found himself increasingly harassed by the memory of a recent encounter during which his wife had unjustly blamed him for something he hadn't done. He knew she wasn't in control of herself and that he shouldn't take it personally, but he couldn't stop himself from obsessively going over and over what she said, what he said, and what he would really like to have said. He could feel his anger and stress levels rising, and no amount of following the breath had any effect on the interior rant that his prayer had become.

The next day, the same thing happened, and again the day after that. Denis just couldn't seem to let go of the incident. Later, he recounted it all to his director despondently.

'If this happens again', his director said, 'sit with it before the Lord. Tell him how angry you feel with your wife. Don't say to yourself that you shouldn't feel angry, that it's not her fault. The fact is, you are angry. Bring that before the Lord and see what happens.'

Denis did as his director suggested. In the presence of God, in that safe place with the One he knew loved him, he allowed himself to feel all the stored up anger and resentment of months.

'I feel sometimes that I hate her,' he told God, 'she is utterly unreasonable.'

Suddenly he found himself in tears, and realised that the anger was covering a huge sense of bereavement. He realised that he had lost the wife he loved; the person he was now living with had changed beyond recognition. His anger, he now realised, was directed more against God, for allowing such a thing to happen, than it was against his wife. He sat there before God in the knowledge that he was angry with him. He was able to admit this to God, knowing that God's love for him would not change. His prayer that day was truer and deeper than it had been for a long time.

Similarly, a seemingly persistent distraction may when examined prove to contain a gift, although not perhaps the gift you expect. I was in the habit of making a directed retreat every year at the same monastery (you can read about directed retreats in chapter 10). Each year, as I walked around the locality, I thought how much I would like to live there. In every way, it would be more convenient than where I lived at the time, but I knew that prices in this locality were much more expensive than in my own, and I couldn't afford to move.

One year, my prayer periods during the retreat were persistently interrupted by a fantasy of living in the area. Annoyed by this useless dream, I mentioned it to my director. He wondered if perhaps God was allowing this to come up in my prayer for a reason.

'Perhaps he wants you to seriously consider moving', my director said.

I took this seriously, and when the retreat was over, I took some financial advice which encouraged me to believe that, if I sold my house, I could in fact afford to purchase a modest property in the area I liked so much. However, I still wasn't sure whether the thought of moving really came from God, or whether it was, in fact, no more than a distraction. So I brought the decision about moving into my prayer, but at the same time, took the necessary practical steps. I put my house on the market. Realising that at last I might be able to fulfil my dream of many years, I began to feel excited about it. I went to see a number of small properties that were for sale in the area that I liked, and was happy to see that if my own house sold for the sum I was looking for, I would be able to buy one of them.

But just at this time, property prices, which had been soaring for years, began to fall. Over the next year I watched my house rapidly decrease in value, while the properties I was interested in buying, although they too decreased, did not do so as rapidly, being in a more desirable area. I saw the gap widen between what I might get for my own house and what I wanted to buy. Months went past. People came to view my house, but no offers were made. People were getting cautious, waiting to see if prices would fall further.

In the meantime, I kept bringing the decision about selling the house and moving home to prayer, asking God to show me clearly where I could best serve him, what decision would lead me to the life and the freedom I knew he desired for me. No great revelation came to me; I heard no voice telling me what to do. Finally, when my house had been on the market for over a year and its value had decreased substantially, I realised that I could not now buy even a small property in the locality I had hoped for. I took my house off the market.

'I wonder what it was all about,' my director said, the next time I went to see him. 'Have you any idea?'

Actually, I had. I had been increasingly struck throughout the year by my own sense of freedom about the whole thing. I knew that no matter what happened, I would be absolutely happy that it was for my greatest good. This was in marked contrast to how I would have been in the past: in those days, when I set my heart on something, I was shattered when the dream fell through.

'This has been a huge gift to me,' I told my director. 'I discovered an inner freedom that I didn't know I had, and a trust in God that was so much stronger than I knew.'

The distraction about buying the house had been God's way of showing me some of the fruits of my years of prayer: freedom and trust, gifts more valuable than the house of my dreams.

If you practice this sort of prayer regularly – ideally, ever day – you will find that your spiritual senses are becoming more finely tuned, so that the silence becomes more and more appealing to you, and so that you can recognise more readily the call of God in the various moments of your life. And in the end, this will grow to such a point that you will find great peace no matter what dramas or tragedies are happening in your life. You will still feel pain and sadness, of course you will, but you will be conscious always of a deep sense of peace and trust.

'For surely I know the plans I have for you,' says the Lord. 'Plans for your welfare and not for your harm, to give you a future with hope'.[24]

You will come to know beyond all doubt that whatever is happening has a purpose, and that purpose is always good. You will realise that God's call is hidden in the events of your life, and you will learn to recognise and respond to it, because it is a loving call, the call of your father, and it will lead always, always, to freedom and to life.

Emotions

People often mistake the arising of emotions – especially negative emotions – in their prayer for distractions. They waste much precious time and energy trying to rid themselves of what they believe are inappropriate feelings of anger, bitterness or sadness. But an emotion is not a distraction, it is simply a feeling that you are having right now. It can, however, lead to a distraction, so it is important both to understand how this happens, and what to do to prevent it, or to remedy it if it occurs.

First of all, an emotion of any kind is a help, not a hindrance, when it arises during prayer. Why do I say this? Well, as you will recall, during prayer, your essential role (and in the later stages, your only role) is to be present. This means not only being physically present, but also mentally, emotionally and spiritually present. In other words, the ideal you are striving for is to be totally grounded in the present moment. This is the purpose of your various stilling and quieting exercises such as following the breath, or the use of the sacred word or mantra.

An emotion is a feeling that arises in you right now, in the present moment. You can't experience an emotion in the past or in the future – all you can do is remember what it felt like, or imagine what it will feel like. Although those thoughts or imaginings may be strong enough to produce an emotion in you, that emotion will always arise now, in the present moment. It is precisely because it is a creature of the present moment that an emotion can be a help during prayer, provided you relate to it in the right way.

So how should you relate to it in a way that will help your prayer? Let's imagine three versions of the same scenario. In each of them our hero, John, will have the same experience of a powerful emotion invading his prayer, but in each case he will handle it differently. Let's see what happens.

The background in each example is the same. John has had a bad day at the office. Feelings ran high at a departmental meeting and that particular colleague who always manages to get under his skin has done it again. By the time the meeting is over, John is fuming, and the only thing that gets him through the rest of the day is the thought of his peaceful prayer time that evening. He knows it will calm him down and that he will get things into perspective again. So ...

Scenario 1
John lights his candle, pulls the curtains and sits on his prayer

stool. He begins to concentrate on his breathing, and gradually a sense of calm steals over him. He relaxes. He drops his guard. Suddenly, without warning, the thought of what that colleague had said to him at the meeting comes back to him, and instantly John is alive with fury. What a fool he was, he thinks. He should have told that guy exactly where he got off. A choice remark he could have made but didn't comes into his mind. He imagines his colleague's reaction if he had said that! Hah! That would have told him alright! John is by now reliving his confrontation with his colleague, but this time saying all the things he hadn't said in reality. His colleague responds in kind, further inflaming John ... A bell rings. What? Confused, John opens his eyes and looks around. The bell was the timer he had set to mark the end of his hour of prayer. The entire hour has been taken up in an imaginary row with his colleague. If anything, John now feels angrier than ever. Not only has his colleague spoiled his day in the office, he has also spoiled his prayer!

Scenario 2

All happens as above, up to the point where John recalls what his colleague had said, and finds himself burning with anger. This is awful, he thinks. I shouldn't be feeling like this. I am in a holy place here, a sacred space. What must God be thinking of me? He tries to calm down his anger by taking a few deep breaths. It works for a couple of seconds, and then back comes the anger again. Really, it seems to be getting even stronger. He feels quite violent towards that colleague. If the guy walked in that door now, God only knows what John would do ... This is dreadful. What's more, it's not the first time it has happened. It seems to John that, of late, almost every time he tries to pray he ends up battling with anger. He wonders if he should try a different method, or maybe give up prayer for a while till things calm down. After all, it can't be much good either to him or to God to spend an hour every evening thinking violent thoughts. His timer rings. The hour is up. John feels totally stressed out from his lost battle with his anger. On top of the anger, he now also feels guilt at the wasted prayer time ...

Scenario 3

John has lit his candle, sat himself on his prayer stool and concentrated on his breathing for a few minutes. Suddenly, remembering how his colleague had treated him at the meeting, he is ablaze with anger. He thinks of something really nasty he could have said to his colleague, something that would have put him in his place once and for all. He takes a deep breath. I am feeling very angry right now, he thinks. He turns to God. Here I am, he says, I am very angry! I do not love my colleague, in fact, I hate him. This is the way I am right now, here in this present moment, as I begin my prayer – or rather, our prayer; for I know there are two of us here. I know that this is a blessed and sacred moment, because you are present to me and I am present to you. I also know that your love for me is unconditional; it makes absolutely no difference to you whether I am in a good humour or a bad one, you love me in the very same way and are glad that I am here with you. Having said that, you don't want me to be imprisoned by my anger. In so far as it is destructive, crippling or incapacitating, or brings pain to myself or others (including my colleague), you want to free me from it. I therefore hold it up to you so that your healing gaze can rest upon it. John rests there, under the healing and loving gaze of God, and feels his anger begin to drain away. If it rises up again, he follows the same procedure, acknowledging it, and bringing it there into his prayer before God. Even if it keeps rising, and he has to go through the same procedure every time, he is conscious at the end of his prayer time of a sense of something being right, truthful. He has not acted the hypocrite before God. He is reminded of the gospel story of the Pharisee and the publican, and knows that, like the publican, he has ended his prayer at rights with God.[25]

Those are the three scenarios. In all of them, John felt violently angry during his prayer time. In the first scenario, his anger led him into thoughts of what he might have said that became a full-blown re-hash of the day's argument, with embellishments. This was a true distraction: John had been dragged completely away from the reality of the present graced moment into a wholly imaginary re-enactment of the day's events. In the second scenario, John was overtaken not only by anger, but also by guilt at having the feeling at all in the first place. This led him to spend the entire time battling unsuccessfully with the anger, trying to make it go away. This too is a true distraction. He is like the father in the example Vincent's director had used earlier, running upstairs in useless attempts to quieten the noisy children, while leaving his guest alone below. Worse still, by the end of the hour, John was seriously entertaining thoughts of giving up prayer altogether – the ultimate distraction of all.

But in the third scenario, John saw in his anger not an obstacle to be avoided, but a doorway into the present moment, into God's presence. He realised that if he acknowledged and really felt his anger, he would be truly anchored in the present moment, because that emotion was precisely what was happening to him and in him now. And we saw how this insight led him to stand there before God in the utter truth of his present anger. In that attitude, he was truly honest, totally himself, and was therefore open to God's healing grace.

The same is true of any emotion that arises during prayer, and not only the negative ones. Joy, for example, can also be a doorway into God's presence, but if not interacted with in that way, can lead to memories of the past or imagination of the future which will distract you from the reality of God's presence here and now.

Helplessness

In the early stages of prayer, as we have already seen, you will have much to occupy you. Part of the time will be taken up by one of the exercises that focuses you on the present, and the remainder with either resting quietly in an awareness of the presence of God, or of his love, or with speaking to him from your heart. Time tends to pass quickly and you have a sense of fulfilment when the period is over. You become accustomed to your prayer time having a certain amount of content, of things happening. If you were to make a note of how it went at the end of the period (and more of this later) you would have much to write.

When prayer begins to move into simplicity, this changes. You are not, as a rule, conscious of much happening during this stage in your prayer. As we have already seen, a lot is in fact happening, but it is happening at a level too deep for your conscious mind, for the most part, to be aware of it. This lack of event, or of content in your prayer, will not always bother you. Part of the change that occurs in you during the transition into simplicity is the ability to rest quietly in God's presence, vaguely conscious of being secretly nourished, although unable to put this into words or even to think clearly about it. There is a sense of 'rightness' once the initial anxiety we spoke about earlier has passed.

But occasionally, something else happens. An alarming feeling of helplessness arises in you as you sit to begin your prayer. This sense of helplessness generally doesn't begin to happen until some time after your prayer has already simplified and you have become accustomed to resting quietly in an inner peace and subtle sense of God's presence. This helplessness is not the same thing as the anxiety you felt when your prayer first began to move into simplicity and you found yourself unable to meditate, or use the sacred word, or concentrate on your breathing. This is something different, although at first often confused with it.

The essential thing that is different about it is that because it occurs after you have abandoned your old methods of praying, it does not give rise to an anxiety about being unable to practice those methods. However, you will feel so disturbed by what is happening that you may not be able to make this distinction. The confusing thing about this new feeling is that it makes you think – just like the transition to the second stage of prayer did – that you must be doing something wrong. However, whereas in that earlier stage, you probably concluded that you weren't meditating properly, or concentrating sufficiently on your breathing or sacred word, this time you don't know what it is that you haven't been doing properly, since you haven't really been doing anything anyway, other than coming faithfully to prayer and spending the allotted time there.

You remember Vincent, he of the thoughts that behaved like unruly children? He described his own experience this way:

'It's as if suddenly I'm locked outside some secret place that I always knew the way into before. And yet, when I ask myself how I got in there at other times, I have to confess that I don't know.'

I asked Vincent what he used to do when he began his prayer during those times.

'Well,' he said, 'I usually began with a prayer to the Holy Spirit, and then I just put myself there before God, in whatever state I happened to be in.'

'And what happened then?' I asked.

Vincent frowned thoughtfully. 'It's hard to say really. Somehow or other, I was just peaceful and content to be there. I seemed to be held there, in a way.'

'And now?' I prodded.

'Now I say the prayer to the Holy Spirit, settle down, and then a wave of panic comes over me. I don't know what to do any more.'

Vincent has said two very significant things in this short excerpt from our conversation. First, he describes his earlier experience as 'being held' and second, he says he doesn't now know what to do. Why are these things significant?

Think about it. If Vincent was indeed being held in prayer, then by definition, he was not holding himself there. If you hold a cup in your hand, the cup is being held there. The cup is not holding itself in your hand. If you let go, the cup will fall. You are in charge.

So the prayer that Vincent had been enjoying up to now was a prayer in which he was not in charge. It was a sheer gift. There was a sense in which Vincent knew this, but as time went on, the human tendency to appropriate everything took over, and he agreed with me that, if asked, he would probably have described himself as 'being able' to enter into a contemplative state of prayer. Imperceptibly, he had become possessive about his prayer. He had to learn that he was not able, that in fact, he was helpless.

The importance of this lesson for you, if you have this experience, cannot be overestimated. It goes to the essence of your liberation, your coming into the fullness of the light of truth. Your union with God, your privilege in being allowed to converse with him, his sharing himself with you in friendship, can never be earned by you. They remain always total gift. Until this fact sinks into the very depth of your being, you will not be able to live in the truth.

So how should you behave, faced with this sense of utter helplessness in prayer, this feeling that you are not praying at all, that you cannot pray?

First, do nothing different. This is all about learning to trust God. As we said at the start, there are two people present at prayer time, you and God, and God is always active, increasing in you his life and his freedom. The fact that you are unaware of that on any conscious level doesn't make it any less true. So stay there, be aware of the discomfort of your feeling of helplessness. As long as you feel that you are helpless, (in the sense of being unable to help yourself, of course; not in the sense of being without any help) you are grounded in the truth. All the months and years when you did not feel helpless were less true than this moment now is. And the closer you are to the truth, the closer you are to God, who is Truth itself.

St Paul's words to the Romans may be of comfort to you now. Speaking of the Holy Spirit, he says,

> Likewise the Spirit helps us in our weakness; for we do not know how to pray as we ought, but that very Spirit intercedes for us with sighs too deep for words. And God, who searches the heart, knows what is in the mind of the Spirit, because the Spirit intercedes for the saints according to the will of God.[26]

So don't panic. You are held safely in God's hands now just as you were at every other stage of your prayer. You are in a good place, a happy place, a place that will lead you ever more surely into freedom and life.

Temptation and failure

However, as long as you are still on this earth, the freedom of God's children that is ours can only be enjoyed in a limited way. You have to wait for the next life to enter fully into that freedom. And so, at this point, I would like to say something very briefly about the place of temptation and failure in your life.

As long as you are alive you will not be free from temptation. If you think that progress in contemplative prayer and in the spiritual life will mean blissful peace and an end to struggle, you are destined to be sadly disappointed. You have only to look at the life of Christ to see that temptation is a part of the human condition. He, as we know, underwent temptation during the forty days he spent in the desert at the start of his public ministry. So you can expect to face it – and to fall – right up to your dying day. But once prayer has taught you to recognise and embrace your weakness, once you have begun to understand that God knows you to your core and loves you exactly as you are, you will have a very different view of temptation. Because you are now familiar with your wounds and weaknesses, you will immediately recognise temptation for what it is, and it will serve you as a reminder to turn to God who is hidden in that very place of your weakness. You will turn to him in the full knowledge that you are weak and that you need him, and in total trust that he loves you even when you fall. So the temptation – and even the fall, if you do fall – will become the cause of turning you even more strongly towards your Father who loves you. In other words, hidden in each temptation is a new invitation, an invitation to prayer, to communion with Jesus and with his Father. And each acceptance of that invitation will bring you again into that Divine embrace, and in each new embrace a little more of God's holiness will be passed to you. So instead of temptation pulling you down, it will raise you up, lifting you each time into the arms of God.

You need humility in order to embrace and welcome weakness and temptation in the way I have described. Humility is a much misunderstood virtue. There is nothing Uriah Heap-like about it, nothing that requires you to go around acting as if you were the lowest of all, behaving like a door-mat. Jesus was humble, but there is nothing in the gospels that gives us the impression of someone who went around giving way to all and sundry under the illusion that he didn't deserve to walk the face of the earth. No, Jesus behaved like the master and teacher he was, yet Paul could say of him

> Who, though he was in the form of God,
> did not regard equality with God
> as something to be exploited,
> But emptied himself,
> taking the form of a slave,
> being born in human likeness.
> And being found in human form,
> he humbled himself
> and became obedient to the point of death –
> death on a cross.[27]

Humility means seeing yourself as you really are, the good and the bad, not grasping the good, not obsessing about the bad, accepting yourself that way in peace, knowing that this is how God sees you, and that he loves you greatly. Unfortunately, humility is often misunderstood, and we find that people frequently think that a sort of judgemental self-loathing is in fact humility. This is not to say that you should not admit your faults and repent of them. Of course you should! But having done that, you should not get bogged down in regrets and recriminations. As Martin Laird says, true humility is the wide open space of self-knowledge that opens onto God.[28]

Failure is part of the search for God. There are very few saints, very few mystics, who have not experienced failure in their efforts on the spiritual path. You sometimes find people who are very drawn to prayer, but are held back because they are unable to come to terms with something in their past. Because they are unable to forgive themselves, they can't believe that God has forgiven them. This is not true repentance, because it keeps such people away from God instead of drawing them towards him. True repentance comes with the realisation that the love of God for you has never wavered for one moment; that the fatted calf, the robe and the ring have always been waiting in the Father's house for the return of the Prodigal child. More than that, Jesus, the Good Shepherd, has been out combing the highways and byways for his lost sheep.

If I may, I'll give you an example of this from my own life. From the age of fifteen, when I first discovered the writings of St John of the Cross and St Teresa of Avila, I felt strongly drawn to a life of contemplative prayer. At that time, I thought the only way to be a contemplative was by entering a contemplative order. I don't think that now – I know now that, although some people are called to live a contemplative life in the most absolute way, by entering a monastery dedicated to that way of life, we are nevertheless all called to be contemplatives. Anyway, when I was eighteen, I joined the Carmelites, a strictly enclosed contemplative order.

At first, all went well, but little by little it became evident to me and to those around me that the strictly enclosed life of a Carmelite in the nineteen sixties was going to prove too difficult for me. But I didn't want to give up. This was what I had longed for since I was fifteen. I battled on until the strain became too much, and my health broke down. That way, of course, I had an 'excuse' for leaving: I wasn't turning my back on my vocation or on my quest, I was being forced to leave by my own health. But although this may have provided me with an excuse that allowed me to leave without losing face, it didn't wash with my own conscience, and I left the convent with an appalling sense of guilt.

Back in the world again, I could find only one way of coping with this guilt, and that was not to think about God at all. This was difficult at first, but like anything, it became easier with practice. I continued to do the things practising Catholics did: I went to Sunday Mass, and to confession every so often, but I no longer prayed because it was too painful. And so the life that I was emptying of God gradually filled up with things that were not God. I began to drift and to lose the impetus that had made me set out in the first place. This state of things lasted for eighteen years. Yes, eighteen years!

And then, one June evening – I was living in Luxembourg at the time – I sat on the balcony of my apartment after dinner to read a book. Some of my favourite music – it was Paul Simon actually – was drifting out on the summer air from the living room. I read the first few pages of the book. Somehow, it wasn't holding my attention. I went back inside to look for something else. Crouched before the bookshelves, I pulled out volume after volume, but nothing appealed. Then a purple-covered paperback at the back of one of the shelves caught my eye. I took it out. It was *The Spiritual Canticle* of St John of the Cross, one of his most beautiful poems. I hadn't looked at it for years. Idly, I opened it at the page where the full text of the famous poem is set out, and read the first lines:

> Whither hast thou hidden thyself, and hast left me,
> O Beloved, to my sighing?
> Thou didst flee like the hart, having wounded me: I went
> out after thee, calling, and thou wert gone.

I can only describe what happened next by saying that suddenly I realised all that I had lost eighteen years earlier, and at the same moment realised that I had never lost it at all, that all the time it had been there for the asking. It was like being told that someone I dearly loved had just died, and while I was trying to take in the fact of their death, they walked into the room, alive. It was desolation and joy at the very same moment. And I realised an immense truth, that although I had given up the search for God, he had never given up the search for me. As John of the Cross himself says: If the soul is seeking its Beloved, how much more is the Beloved seeking the soul!

That experience, an experience of the inexhaustible and faithful love of God for me, revived in me all the dying and dead embers of my first love, and I set out once more on the quest, full of renewed hope.

To conclude, the regular practice of prayer brings you first to an awareness of your inner wounds, then to an acceptance of them, and finally to embracing them as you realise that they are the doorway by means of which God comes to you. In this embrace, you yourself are embraced by God, and in the light that shines from his holy face, you recognise that your wounds have been transfigured and made glorious by Jesus, your Saviour, who in dying has taken on your wretchedness and your misery, your poverty and your pain.

CHAPTER SIX

Reviewing your Prayer

Your prayer time will always be full of event, although this will not always be evident to you at the time. Sometimes, indeed, it will seem to you like one big non-event. But, as I've said a number of times, there are two people involved in your prayer: you, and God, and God is always active. But, as we've seen, for various reasons, God's activity isn't always evident to your conscious mind.

Nevertheless, there is always something to be learned from every prayer period, and often that only becomes clear later. You can help this process along by reviewing your prayer.

There are two ways of reviewing your prayer: prayerful reflection and journalling. We'll look at each of these in turn.

Prayerful reflection

This involves taking some time shortly after your prayer period. First, take a short break: have a cup of coffee, or take a brief walk. Then sit down, close your eyes, ask the Holy Spirit to guide your reflection and to bring to your mind anything God wants you to learn from your prayer period.

Think first about how you were on beginning your prayer. Were you calm, agitated, sad, happy, tired? Perhaps you were angry about something that had happened, or excited about some future event. Whatever state you were in, recall it now.

Next, how did you begin? Did you use an opening prayer? What was it? Relive it now. Then consider your focusing exercise. What did you use? Was it imaginative meditation on a scene from scripture? Was it following your breathing? Or was it a mantra, or the use of a sacred word? Whatever it was, relive it now, and consider how you felt as you did it.

If your focusing exercise was an imaginative reflection on scripture, how did it go for you? Were you able to enter fully into the scene you had chosen? If so, how did it develop? Did you feel any emotion arising in you? Were you moved to speak to God? If so, what did you say? Were you aware of any response?

If you followed the breath, how was that for you? Did it lead you quickly into stillness, or did you find it difficult to concentrate? If so, can you identify why? Was it because something earlier in the day had bothered you? Or was there some other reason? Follow the same procedure if your exercise was a mantra or the sacred word.

Then recall how your prayer developed. Did you need to use the exercise all the way through, or were there periods where you had a sense of being held in peace? Did anything else happen? Did you experience any overflow, or sense of God's presence? If you experienced nothing at all, take note of that, for it, too, is an event!

Finally, consider how you ended your prayer, and how you felt when the alarm clock rang, or whatever other signal you had set to tell you the time was up happened. Were you relieved, disappointed, surprised, what? You may be very surprised now when you recall your feeling. When Anne, a woman I know, first did this exercise at a time when her prayer felt very dry and even, as she said herself, boring, she was utterly astonished to discover that her reaction to the clock going off had been 'Oh no, an hour surely can't be up already? I don't want to end yet!' She had to acknowledge then that there must have been a lot more going on during her prayer than she was aware of.

Journalling

Journalling is a process very similar to prayerful reflection, except that you write everything down. Some people are more comfortable with putting their thoughts down on paper than in trying to hold them, as it were, in their heads. There is also the added advantage that, because it is naturally a slower process, and takes more time than prayerful reflection, you may find that you can recall your prayer in greater detail.

Another advantage of this process is that, if you do it regularly, you build up gradually a written picture of your prayer over time, which can be of great assistance to you in seeing where it is going, and in identifying areas where you might benefit from a discussion with your spiritual director.

CHAPTER SEVEN

Living your New Life

Your prayer has been gradually changing your life. As it develops, so too will your new life unfold; a life in which you are beginning to taste the freedom of the children of God. In this chapter, we look at some of the ways in which your old, hardened attitudes are changing, and at the freedom and happiness those changes are bringing you.

Standing unprotected before God

I have already mentioned a few times Sister Wendy Beckett's definition of prayer as 'standing unprotected before God'. This simple definition of prayer is, however, anything but simple to put into practice. Learning to take up this attitude is the work of a lifetime, but the effort will be infinitely rewarding. For in learning to stand unprotected before God, you must of necessity abandon all your defences. This is slow work; it is the traditional work of the spiritual combat described by the great mystical writers of every generation. It is mainly God's work, but it requires your assent and co-operation at every stage.

When a small child prays, it stands before God unprotected. This is one of the many reasons why Jesus recommended that we should become like little children. But we adults come to him all dressed up, in a strange imitation of the dressing-up games that children love to play. Children, however, are wiser in this matter than we are: they know they are only pretending to be princesses or Superman or other TV heros. But we, sad fallen children of Eve that we are, do not even realise that we are pretending. When you don the masks that hide you from others and very often from yourself, you think that they are your own true face. You stand before God concealed behind your mask, holding a shield before your body to protect you from him.

Wendy Beckett does us a huge favour in defining prayer as she does. In trying to put what she urges upon you into practice, you are forced to recognise how far from being unprotected you are. And of course in this very act of recognition, the battle is already joined. It is a well-known fact that denial is one of the greatest defences the mind can erect; with the recognition that you are in denial you have already moved forward into a place of huge growth.

Abandoning your defences
But, being practical about it, how can you begin the work of standing unprotected before God in prayer? You can begin by wanting to do so – or, if you can't do that, by wanting to want to do so. You then can ask for God's help to enable you to come before him in utter truth – which is just another way of saying 'unprotected', because all your defences are lies – and you can be absolutely certain that God will answer this prayer, because it is in accordance with the mind of God, in whom there is no darkness and no shadow of deceit.

The 'trustful face' mask
And then you must be vigilant, and must learn to recognise your own secret defences. For with the best will in the world, it is a terrifying thing to stand unprotected before the Living God. Sooner or later during your period of prayer, your attitude of humility and openness will change into a defensiveness that can take many forms. In some of its forms, you will recognise it straight away: it can, for example, manifest itself as a sort of *caveat* that introduces itself into your declared desire to do only God's will. You begin to point out to God that, although you are of course willing to give up your various attachments, you know that he can't want you, for the moment, to give up that particular person, or work, or form of prayer, because to do so would be bad for your health / sanity / spiritual well-being …

And when you examine this process more closely, you are led to another revelation: you don't really trust God. God only knows what God might do if you really let go of control! You are not convinced at gut level that he has your best interests at heart. It can be a great shock to people who have lived a serious spiritual life to come up against this truth about themselves. But, three cheers! That is one mask gone already! Now, minus your 'trustful face' mask, you can stand before God acknowledging that you do not fully trust him. God, of course, knew that already: you were the only one who was fooled. Now you are beginning to emerge into the light of the truth.

The defence against inactivity

Other defences are more subtle. There is, for example, the need to feel that you are doing something during prayer, and this can lead you to fill the emptiness of a dry prayer with activity. Here there is need for careful discernment. In the early days of your prayer life, activity, in the form of meditation or other 'centering' method which helps to still you and focus you is, as we have seen, usually necessary. But as prayer moves on into simplicity, a simple 'being there' is normally what God requires, as he is feeding you with secret food not readily accessible to the senses. This is when you truly begin to stand unprotected before him, but it is also the time when that insidious shield of 'doing' inserts itself between you and God. I seem to be doing nothing, so I can't be praying, you think. So you pick up a book, or you try to meditate on a passage of scripture, all the time effectively blocking the secret inflow of God.

The defence against the transcendence of God

Another subtle defence comes into its own after some profound prayer experience – perhaps it was an experience of God's indwelling or of his special love for you, or of the union of all creation in him. Whatever it was, it filled you with overwhelming joy at the time, and yet, curiously, you somehow or other find it difficult to get down to prayer again. When your next prayer time comes around, you are perhaps very busy, or very tired, or just not in the right mood. And before you know where you are, you have missed or cut short several prayer periods.

Frank is a case in point. A few years ago, he felt that his prayer life seemed to have fallen into a rut. Prayer time was filled with activity – with reading and making notes and occasionally praying for other people. But somehow, something was lacking. I asked about periods of silence in his prayer. There were none. A little probing revealed that over twenty years earlier, Frank had had a profound experience during prayer of God's unconditional love for him. So deeply had the experience impressed him that he could still recall exactly where he was, and the time of day at which it had happened. Also, he remembered that at that time, his usual practice during prayer was to sit in stillness. He had never done it since. Why not? A little probing revealed a deep-seated belief that the Christian life couldn't be just 'sitting around enjoying yourself with nice feelings', as he put it. Pressed further, Frank admitted that he had found the experience so overwhelming that he felt that if it happened again, it might affect his sanity. So he had carefully guarded against any such eventuality by filling his prayer up with activity. God hadn't a hope of being heard.

What is happening in such a situation? You are defending yourself against an overpowering experience which, joyful as it was to your outward senses, has in the end been an experience, however tiny, of the transcendence of God. You may not realise it, but inside you are terrified. Think of the passages in the New Testament where various people had some sort of epiphany – their reaction was a mixture of joy and fear. At the Annunciation, the angel had to reassure Mary, 'Fear not, Mary!' At the Transfiguration, Peter, James and John felt, on the one hand, that it was so good for them to be there that they wanted to build three tabernacles, but on the other hand, they fell to the ground in terror when the voice spoke from the cloud, even though the voice was speaking words of comfort: 'This is my beloved Son!' Recognising that this happens quite commonly is a great help in identifying and abandoning that particular defence.

The defence against an unwelcome demand

At other times, you may become vaguely aware that God is asking something of you that you feel unable to face. Again your
defence will be either to stay away from prayer or to fill it up
with reading or some other activity – anything to blot out that
insistent small voice. Yet, paradoxically, it is only in prayer that
you will get the strength to face the thing you are afraid of. The
wonderful thing about being unprotected before God is that, in
taking possession of you, God does all for you. You no longer
have to rely on your own strength, nor fear your own weakness.

All of these defences – and many more: you will learn to
recognise your own special and particular ones – prevent you
from standing unprotected before God. They have to be abandoned, until you are able to come to prayer and stand before
your Father as Jesus did, in utter trust. In his passion and in his
death, Jesus was the great and shining example of what it means
to stand absolutely unprotected before God. Looking at Jesus in
the garden of Gethsemane, we see what it truly means to take up
that attitude. We see a man confessing in total honesty to God
his weakness and terror, his seeming inability to face what lay
before him. We see him lying on the ground, sweating blood in
the agony of his horror. He is totally vulnerable, totally exposed,
totally unprotected. God can do what he likes with this man.
Jesus is at his mercy. He begs God not to ask him to face the
nightmare ahead, and yet he does not, like us, put up defences.
He could have done so: there were very many excellent argu-
ments as to why he needed to live longer. He could have said
that it would be better for everyone if he stayed alive and continued his mission. So many people had heard the good news, but
so many others still needed to hear it. Many people had been
healed, but very many more were ill. Jesus was only a young
man: if he had done so much in a short time, how much more
would he be able to do given a long life, and all for the glory of
the Father and the coming of his kingdom. He could have pointed
to the inadequacy of the miserable little group that would have
to take over the mission of announcing the kingdom of God, and

who were even now asleep a short distance away, unable to keep him company in his loneliness. These things would have been true, and they must, even then, have seemed important to Jesus. Yet his trust in his Father, even at that moment of agony and of the seeming collapse of everything, never faltered, and it was this trust which enabled him to open his arms and bare to the Father's love his defenceless heart. 'Yet, not my will, but thine be done.'

Later, when the horror was almost played out, when he was stretched on the cross between two criminals, when all that he had lived for was held up to ridicule and mockery, when he had been stripped of his clothes, his dignity, and even apparently of his God, this defenceless man cried out his abandonment, and then delivered up to his Father all that remained to him: his spirit. Into your hands I commend my spirit. O Jesus, teach us to stand with you in utter truth and trust before your Father and ours, so that with you we may come to the glory and joy of his kingdom and take our place there with you as his dearly beloved children, Amen.

Unknowing the God you thought you knew

In the Book of Exodus we read that while Moses was on Mount Horeb, receiving the Ten Commandments from God, the children of Israel, growing weary of waiting for him, fashioned a calf from molten gold and began to worship it.[29] They knew, of course, that the golden calf wasn't God, but they needed an image of God. They found it very difficult to pray to a God that they could neither see nor hear. The problem with images, of course, is that after a while you begin to believe that the image is the truth. You saw this in the previous chapter in relation to images of yourself: you genuinely believed that they were you.

When Moses finally came down from the mountain and saw what the Israelites had done, he was furious. Pulling the golden calf from its pedestal, he flung it to the ground, where it shattered in pieces. We saw in chapter 4 how something similar happens to the false images of ourselves as we progress in prayer:

little by little, cracks appear. A piece of plaster falls off here, a hole appears there, until whole pieces fall away and the true and beautiful face of the child of God appears beneath.

Something similar has to happen with regard to our image of God for, like the Israelites, every single one of us has fashioned for ourselves a Golden Calf, an image of God that is not God, because no image can possibly represent all that God is in himself.

When you practise prayer seriously, you come to realise that the spiritual journey towards union with God consists in large part of a stripping from you of everything that is not God. It is, of course, God himself who undertakes this work, who strips you of everything to which you are attached, so that empty, light and unencumbered, you are ready finally to be united with him. The poet Francis Thompson described it well.

> My harness piece by piece Thou hast hewn from me,
> And smitten me to my knee;
> I am defenceless utterly.
> I slept, methinks, and woke,
> And, slowly gazing, find me stripped in sleep.

We don't have too much difficulty in understanding the necessity for this process: we are creatures of attachment and we search for the happiness we are destined for in all the wrong places. Things stick to you, even when you know that they are not good for you. They bind you around like Elastoplast, these sticky attachments; they encompass you and take away your freedom. They become your prison: a prison of your own making. But as you journey on in prayer, you notice changes in yourself, new ways of looking at things, a desire for greater simplicity that makes it easier for you to abandon the luxuries that at one time you thought you could not do without.

There are different kinds of attachment. First, there is that most extreme form of attachment: addiction. You do not have to be a person of prayer to recognise that an addiction to drugs, alcohol, sex or anything else is a destroyer of freedom and ultimately of physical life. It is clear to us that we cannot be whole until we are freed from such a deadly attachment. However, it is not so immediately apparent that lesser attachments to material things: to money, to possessions, to food and drink, are slowly killing your inner freedom and life. But when you embark upon a life of serious prayer, you quickly come to see the disorder in these attachments, and it is easy enough for any praying person to understand that they are not compatible with union with God. As God takes a hand and begins to set you free, your life moves into greater simplicity and your overwhelming feeling is of liberation and gratitude.

Other attachments are more subtle; even for the praying person it is not always quite so easy to see that they too are hindrances on your journey. You need the light and guidance of the Holy Spirit to enable you to discern when your love for another person, for example, is no longer love but an imprisoning attachment. And even when you are able to see it, you are often powerless to take any remedial action. Here too the stripping takes place, and in this case it can be – and usually is – bitterly painful. The beloved person may be taken from you by death, by illness, by physical separation, by painful misunderstanding. It is very difficult to go on trusting God in such circumstances, particularly when the person is a spouse or other life partner, or a child. It may be hard for you to believe that this is something life-giving. Yet in time, prayer will reveal why it was necessary, will show you the 'invisible worm' that had made the rose sick.

More subtle still is your attachment to spiritual things; yet these too can be your prison, locking you up and keeping you from travelling further on the journey to union with God. 'That can't be God's will!' you protest, when your efforts to do good in your parish or your community are frustrated or made impossible through misunderstanding or poor health, when your efforts to pray meet with dryness and distraction. Sometimes a life choice that you believed to have been wholly for God, such as the choice of the religious life, can be taken from you by your inability to live it out. These are things that are difficult to understand, more difficult still to accept. Yet prayer and reflection in an attitude of openness to God will invariably bring you to the realisation that in some way you had put these choices in the place of God, like the idols the Israelites worshipped in the desert. They are your false gods: you invest your happiness in them rather than in the God to whom they should lead you. And so, in order to be united with him, you must lose your attachment to everything that is not him. That much you can at least grasp.

The real shock comes when you begin to realise that you must lose God himself – you must lose, that is, the God you thought you knew. Because of course, the God you think you know cannot be God as he really is, simply because God is infinite and your finite mind cannot comprehend the infinite.

Almost all of us will have experienced the loss of our childhood images of God, and this will not have worried us in any way. It happens quite naturally as we grow up, as we begin to pray more and to read the scriptures. As a child, you probably had some rather anthropomorphic image of God – a benign old man with a white beard perhaps, or a loving father a bit like your own earthly one, maybe a rather cross teacher ready to pounce on the slightest fault. You grew out of these as you grew out of other childhood images and attachments, and they were replaced with what you considered to be more 'adult' images of God: a loving God, or a demanding God or even a vulnerable God. The list is endless and your adult images of God are often drawn from scripture or from other spiritual reading. People who pray, people who take seriously the spiritual life, become much attached to these images. 'God is for me a loving God', you often hear people say, for example, or: 'I see God as a just God.' They would not want to change that image of him, if asked to do so.

Yet, to say that God is a loving God, or a just God, or even both together, does not describe God. God is a loving God, yes; we believe that, and indeed Jesus has told us so. Jesus has also told us that God is just. But that is not all God is. If it was, he would be limited, and then he would not be God. And so it is that, wishing to be all in all to you, he works away at these attachments too, the attachments to images of him, images which in the end will be just as truly 'false gods' as were our addictions, our attachments to money and possessions, to people and places and ways of living. These attachments to your idea of God must also be stripped from you so that you can come to him in his essence, come to him in truth, and so reach the fullness of life and love that he has destined you for. Again, Francis Thompson explains what is happening:

> All that I took from thee I did but take not for thy harms,
> but just that thou might'st seek it in my arms.

When the process of the purification of your idea of God begins to take place, it can be deeply unsettling. This is because, unlike the earlier experience of replacing childhood images of God with adult images, this new process consists in stripping away the adult images *without putting anything in their place*. You must 'unlearn' God; you must 'unknow' him.

People often become aware for the first time that this most profound spiritual purification is happening when the word 'God' ceases to have any meaning for them. They look at it on the page before them, and it simply seems wrong. It suggests nothing to them that coincides in any way with what they experience during prayer. In fact, it suggests nothing at all. It is just a rather odd word, a random collection of letters. The pronoun 'he' also seems wrong in relation to this mysterious being, this Holy One, who you can no longer conceive of as masculine, but then so too does the pronoun 'she', for you cannot think of this entity as feminine either. The neutral word 'it' is clearly wrong. Nothing fits anymore. Who or what is it that you are drawn to? Who or what is the Being that we call God? This is the beginning of your unknowing of God, the beginning of the great void that you must face and through which you must travel if you are to come to union with the Most Holy One in this life.

Why must you 'unknow' the Divinity in this way? The answer is simple: because you cannot possibly know him.[30]

For as the heavens are higher than the earth,
So are my ways higher than your ways,
And my thoughts than your thoughts.[31]

And

For who has known the mind of the Lord? Or who has been his counsellor?[32]

In order to approach the Holy One who is the essence of truth, you must abandon everything that is not the truth. Nothing that you can imagine can be anything like God. No matter what your image of him is, no matter what the word 'God' may have suggested to you, it cannot be the truth. And if it is not true, then the nearer you approach to the Holy One the more your idea of God will jar and create inner discord. That is why you must lose it.

But because nothing comes to replace the old images, you then find that are face to face with nothing, with a void – with *the* Void. This is a terrifying place to be, because it seems to strike at the very heart of your faith. It can seem indeed, at first, to be the very negation of faith. Is there, then, nothing? Is that what you have been journeying towards? Is that what all your yearning has been leading you to? Nothing?

The answer is literally 'yes', because the Most Holy is not any thing that has been created. Therefore, in the most literal sense he is *No Thing* – nothing. And yet, there is a paradox here, as there is in so many of the things of God. For although the Holy One can truly be said to be No Thing, he is also All, the Beginning and the End, Alpha and Omega. You cannot under- stand this until you have faced that Void, and entered it. For it is the testing place of your trust in God, the place where you can say with Job, 'Even if he slays me I will trust him.'[33]

But where can you ever find the courage and the faith to bring yourself to the point of such an heroic act of trust? How can you enter the Void, once you have come face to face with it? The answer is the same as the answer to that other great ques- tion: 'Who will deliver me from this body of death?' Jesus Christ, our Lord, says St Paul, answering this question.[34]

The answer is, Jesus. When you have come to this unsettling, destabilising place on the journey, when you have at last fully realised that the Divinity is totally incomprehensible, utterly Other, then the thought of Jesus comes to you as comfortingly and as familiarly as a warm fire in the middle of winter. Jesus is your Way through the Void, the only one of our kind to have truly known the Most Holy One. Jesus is your Truth, in this bleak desert where you have lost all your half-truths. Jesus is your Life, in what may seem to you to be the valley of death.

> It is my Father who glorifies me, he of whom you say. 'He is our God', though you do not know him. But I know him: if I were to say that I do not know him, I would be a liar like you. But I do know him and I keep his word.[35]

You will probably only begin to realise the gift God has given you in Jesus when you reach this lonely and fearful place where only Jesus is still recognisable. In the darkness of the night of your unknowing of God, Jesus is there with you as your light. He, a human being who nevertheless is God, comes to tell you out of his own experience that you have nothing to fear, that the very hairs of your head are numbered, that you can walk without fear across a void that will bring you to your heart's desire. He tells you that he is with you, that he will never leave you alone. He tells you that he wants you to be with him where he is, with the Father, with the Holy One. He tells you that you can trust him, because everything he says he has first heard from his Father.

This time of your unknowing of God is the time for you to take up the gospels and to seek to know Jesus more and more deeply. An attachment to Jesus is the one attachment that cannot hurt you and that will not be taken from you. You can count on that, for you have God's own word on it:

This is my Son, my Chosen; listen to him![36]

There is no need for you to be afraid. There is no need for you to begin to imagine that you have lost your faith. When thoughts like these come then you must think of Jesus. You must turn to him – for he is alive – and tell him how you feel. He understands, he is like you in everything except sin. He knows what fear is. He knows what the apparent loss of God feels like. Remember his cry on the cross – My God, why have you forsaken me? He knows what it is to be human, but he also knows what it is to be divine, and that is why he is the bridge across the Void, the bridge to the Father, to the Holy One with whom he lives and reigns, in the unity of the Holy Spirit, for ever.

Being healed

You are born to have life, and to be free. Yet so many of us are in pain, are in a sort of half death, are imprisoned in an inner prison that we cannot break out of. We are a wounded people. Psalm 147 tells us this:

> The Lord heals the broken-hearted and binds up every one of your wounds.

These are beautiful and consoling words, but what do they mean? I would like at this point to spend some time reflecting with you on this, and in particular, I would like to consider the role of Jesus, the healer of your inner wounds.

You know from your reading of the gospels that when Jesus lived among us here on earth, he healed the illnesses of many people. Jesus went about doing good, we are told. Why did Jesus heal people's illnesses? You know that his mission on earth was to bring you the good news that the Father loved you, that you are his child, and that the kingdom of heaven was near at hand. This was the constant theme in Jesus' preaching, and strictly speaking, there was no need for him to cure anyone. So why did he do it?

There are at least two reasons that I can think of. One is that the miracles he performed were a sign to everyone that he was sent from God and that therefore they could – and should – listen to him with confidence. But the other reason springs from the very nature of Jesus himself: he was filled with sadness and compassion for all those who were in any sort of pain, or who were in some way unfree.

There are many passages in the gospel that reveal this trait of Jesus. To pick out just a few, there was the deep sadness he felt on hearing of the death of Lazarus, there was the compassion he felt for the widow at Naim who had lost her son and for Jairus whose daughter had died. For all of these, Jesus felt human empathy: he wanted to ease their pain, relieve them of their burden and bring them into freedom.

This is the desire of Jesus for all of us: to bring us life and to bring us into freedom. I came, he said, that they may have life, and that they may have it to the full.[37] We are all broken, we are all wounded, and many of us are half dead. Very few of us are free. You, like the rest of us, long to be whole. You desire to be free from pain, from anxiety and worry. You want to be free of your addictions and of the many cares that hem you in. You want to find peace and joy and life.

The good news is that God wants all of this for you even more than you want it for yourself. During his life on earth, Jesus revealed the secret of the Father's heart many times and in many different circumstances. God's desire for you is that you should enter fully into freedom, fully into life.

For I know the plans I have for you, says the Lord. They are plans for good and not for disaster, to give you a future and a hope.[38]

If this is true – and it is – how is it that so many good people, so many spiritual people, so many people who pray, are burdened with the pain and the imprisonment of their own inner wounds? Why have they not been healed? Why have you not been healed?

I suspect that for many people, healing means the absence of struggle and pain. We would like our inner selves to be beautifully cleaned up, all wounds removed. But is that really what healing means? Look for a moment at Jesus. He was, as you know, wounded for our sins. During the passion and crucifixion, he was wounded externally by the whipping, by the nails and by the lance, and internally when all his friends and even, it seemed, God, had abandoned him. In the garden at Gethsemane, Jesus cried out in terror and anguish, begging God to save him from what lay ahead. On the cross, it seemed that not only had God not heard his prayer, but that he had abandoned him totally. My God, my God, why have you forsaken me?[39]

But after the resurrection, what happened? He appeared to his friends on a number of occasions. Usually they didn't recognise him at first. Apparently his risen body was so different from his earthly, physical body that even those closest to him were initially deceived by it. Mary Magdalene took him to be the gardener. The two disciples on the road to Emmaus thought he was a stranger. There were two methods employed by Jesus in order to make his friends recognise him: one was the breaking of bread, which reminded them of what he had done at the last supper. In this way, the two disciples at Emmaus recognised him.[40] But the second way in which Jesus made himself known to the disciples was by showing them the marks left by his wounds.[41] I believe that this is a very important point: although the wounds were healed, the marks remained.

On Holy Saturday night every year, the Easter Candle is lit from the newly blessed Easter Fire. This is a wonderfully dramatic ceremony. It takes place in darkness, and weather permitting, out of doors. Because of the glorious pageantry of the ceremony, you might miss a symbolic act that takes place just before the candle is lit. The celebrant etches a cross into the candle and inserts five grains of incense into the cross at five places – top, bottom, each arm and centre – to symbolise the five places in Jesus' body where he was wounded: the head, feet, each hand, and side. While he is doing this, the celebrant says the following prayer: 'By his holy and glorious wounds may Christ our Lord guard us and keep us.' The wounds of Jesus have not disappeared; they have become holy and glorious.

What has made them so? The incense placed on the candle gives a hint. Incense symbolises divinity. The wounds of Jesus have become holy and glorious because of their contact with his divinity. And in the same way, it is in their contact with Jesus that your inner wounds will be healed, not by being taken away, as if by some form of divine cosmetic surgery, but by their transformation into the doorways through which God comes to unite you with himself.

Look for a moment more closely at this idea. First of all, let's be clear what I am talking about when I speak about your inner wounds. I am talking about all those afflictions of mind and heart and spirit that imprison you, keep you unfree and prevent you from journeying with joy towards God. I am talking about the things that cause you more suffering even than the pains of the body. I am talking above all of the things of which you are deeply ashamed, the things you share with few, if any, of your friends, the things that are the root of sin in your life.

What are these things? To take some examples, first there are wounds of the mind: depression, anxiety, panic attacks and feelings of worthlessness, illnesses such as schizophrenia, anorexia and many more. Then there are addictions of all sorts: to alcohol, to drugs, to a mixture of both, to food, to starvation, to gambling, to sex ... the list is endless. People can be addicted to practically anything. It doesn't really matter what you are addicted to; what matters is that your addictions imprison you and keep you locked within the four walls of their demands, so that you feel unable to move out into the glorious freedom of the children of God. Or you might have wounds which result from a lack of love during your childhood. Perhaps you were abused, physically or emotionally, or both. Perhaps your parents' own wounds were too great to allow them to nurture you in the way you needed. Perhaps you grew up with a feeling of worthlessness, a belief that you were bad and did not deserve to be loved. Perhaps you were never able to accept and love yourself, much less allow anyone else to do so.

Or maybe your wounds are the result of a life of sin – a life of sin which you feel unable to escape from, or for which, although you have put it behind you, you think you cannot be forgiven.

As you can see from that brief list, our wounds can be many and various. But whatever their nature, they restrict the movement of your deepest self towards God, until the day comes when they are transformed, like those of Jesus, into wounds that are holy and glorious.

How is this to happen? Well, the first thing you have to do is to face the fact of your own woundedness. As long as you continue to run away from the sight of what you believe to be your own ugliness, you will not be healed. Remember St Paul. In his second letter to the Corinthians, he tells how he suffered for a long time from some affliction – he doesn't explain what it was, other than to say it was a thorn in the flesh, a messenger from Satan sent to prevent him from becoming elated at the wonderful revelations he was receiving at the time. Because he says it was sent to stop him from becoming proud, we can, I think, assume that it was something which reminded him that he was human and weak. Anyway, whatever it was, he tells us that he asked the Lord three times to take it away from him. He didn't like it. He didn't like the image of himself that he saw when he looked at it. He wanted to be rid of it, so that he could be clean and pure and suitably attired to be in God's presence. But God did not take it away; instead, Paul heard the Lord say to him: My grace is sufficient for you, for my strength comes to perfection where there is weakness.[42] And then Paul embraced his wounds fully, crying out:

> Gladly therefore will I glory in my weaknesses, so that the power of Christ may dwell in me. For when I am weak, then I am strong![43]

This is what you, too, need to do. But before you can gain the insight that Paul gained – that your wounds are your glory, because they draw to you the power of Christ – you must recognise that you *are* wounded, and you must recognise in what way you are wounded. You can only do this through prayer.

The kind of prayer which will bring you face to face with your wounds is silent prayer, or contemplative prayer. This is the kind of prayer in which God speaks to you, whereas in vocal prayer, you speak to God. When you pray in this way, by simply remaining in silence before God, aware of being in his presence and totally surrendered to his action, little by little the eyes of your heart will begin to see things in their truth, as they really are. And this includes seeing yourself with all your flaws, sins and wounds. It can be a devastating experience at first, but it is of the most vital importance. Until you are able to see yourself as you really are, you will not be able to embrace and welcome your wounds. At this point, you might find yourself tempted to abandon prayer, or at least, silent prayer, and sadly, some people do give up when they reach this stage. When they begin to see themselves as they are, they make a huge mistake. This mistake is to think that the self they now see, the self covered in wounds, is a new development. They think they were never like this in the past, that somehow or other they have got worse since they began to pray. And so they think prayer is not for them, and they give it up.

But of course, nothing new has happened. They were always covered in wounds – they just couldn't see it. Up to that point, the eyes of their heart – their inner eyes – had been glued shut. Now those eyes are open, and they begin to see ourselves as God has always seen them. When this happens to you, celebrate! Call in your friends and open a bottle of wine. You are beginning to enter into the truth which, as Jesus promised, will make you free. If instead of running away, you continue to stand there before God with faith and trust, you will come to a moment of great importance, a moment of realisation. That realisation is that God loves you just as you are, and has always loved you, because he has always seen you just as you are. It is the moment when you can pray Psalm 139 with real understanding:

> You have searched me, Lord, and you know me,
> You know when I sit and when I stand
> For it was you who fashioned my inmost parts,
> who knit me together in my mother's womb.
> Before ever a word is on my lips,
> you know it O Lord, through and through.
> How precious to me are your thoughts O God!
> How vast is the sum of them!

This moment is the beginning of the healing and transforming of your wounds. This is the moment when you can begin, like St Paul, to glory in your infirmities.

However, as Martin Laird says in his book *Into the Silent Land*, this moment often feels more like breakdown than breakthrough.[44] There is real pain involved in facing up before God to your sinfulness and brokenness. It may be that you have spent your life in denial up to that point. We are all very good at constructing pleasing self-images. They may not fool other people, but they fool us. But at this moment, the self-images are revealed for what they are, lying masks. What you need to remember at this moment is that for Christians, resurrection and crucifixion go together. There is no resurrection without a prior crucifixion, but Good Friday is always followed by the glory of Easter Sunday.

The liturgy of Good Friday contains the following passage from the Prophet Isaiah:

See, my servant shall prosper;
he shall be exalted and lifted up
and shall be very high.
Out of his anguish he shall see light;
he shall find satisfaction through his knowledge.

Out of his anguish he shall see light. That extraordinary statement holds the key to the healing that Jesus will bring to your inner wounds. You must go fully into the darkness in order to be able to see the light. Think of day and night: we would never appreciate the beauty of dawn if it did not emerge from the darkness of night. So too you need to embrace the darkness, embrace your wounds, fully accept them, before the transformation can begin. The reason you must not avoid them is because it is precisely in them that you will find God. God in Christ has drawn close to your wounds, and it is in that place of pain and suffering in your life that he embraces you. As Thomas Merton once said, [Jesus] has taken upon himself our wretchedness and our misery; our poverty and our sins[45] ... Like the grains of incense in the Easter Candle, the presence of Christ in the wounded places of your being will transform your wounds, making them holy and glorious.

Through the practice of silent, contemplative prayer, you will learn, sometimes slowly and painfully, how to stay in that place of your woundedness, where God is. As you embrace and accept your wounds, so at the same time you accept and embrace the God who is in that wounded place. And God embraces you, and from that mutual embrace the life of God flows into your death, and the healing of God flows into your sickness, and the freedom of God flows into your captivity. In that place of hurt, whatever it may be – that addiction, that self-loathing, that deep depression, that childhood abuse, that aching bitterness that is left after someone you once loved has betrayed you – in that very place, Jesus will take you by the hand to lead you into freedom.

CHAPTER EIGHT

Food for the Journey

Once your deepest self has been set free, you yourself are also set free to embark upon a wonderful journey. You will have many adventures along the way, and you will expend a lot of energy. To keep up your energy you will need plenty of good food, and like all people who travel, you will be anxious to find someone who will listen to the tales of your adventures. From time to time too you will need to consult your map, and check with someone else that you are reading it correctly and haven't inadvertently strayed off the route. In this chapter, we will look at where you can find the food to keep you going.

Your prayer will by now be feeding you interiorly with a hidden knowledge of God. At times, as we have seen, that secret wisdom may emerge into your consciousness, filling you with joy. But for much of the time that won't be happening. So your conscious self will need something to feed on, something that will be in harmony with what is happening at the deepest level, something that will help you to make sense of the seemingly inexplicable. That something is spiritual reading.

There are two kinds of spiritual reading, and both of them are good. I intend in this chapter to say something about each of them. One kind of reading is, however, essential, and it is of this that I want to speak first. This is the prayerful reading of scripture, sometimes known as *lectio divina* or divine reading.

Lectio divina

The prayerful and faith-filled reading of scripture is a means of feeding your souls with the very word of God. Scripture reading is prayerful when you approach it with the same spirit of reverence with which you have learned to approach your prayer, and it is faith-filled when you believe four things about it: first, that it is the word of God, through which he reveals himself to you; second, that in the scriptures, you have a genuine meeting with the risen Jesus, who is truly present in his Word; third, that it will feed you, that you do not live on bread alone, but 'on every word that comes from the mouth of God'[46] and fourth, that exposure to the Word of God will change you, because –

> the word of God is something alive and active: it cuts more incisively than any two-edged sword: it can seek out the place where soul is divided from spirit, or joints from marrow; it can pass judgement on secret emotions and thoughts.[47]

Scripture reading of this kind should be engaged in regularly, if only for ten minutes. You wouldn't miss dinner on a regular basis: neither should you miss the food of God's word. One is essential for the strength of your body, the other for that of your soul. However, except in the early stages of your prayer life, my own view is that it is not a good idea to use part of your prayer-time for this, simply because it involves a certain amount of reflection, and as we have seen, when your prayer has developed to a certain stage, God takes over and does all the work. In those circumstances, reflection, even on scripture, may be a hindrance rather than a help during your prayer time. So choose some time other than your prayer time for this exercise.

Begin your reading by choosing a passage of scripture. It's better not to choose too lengthy a piece, or you will simply get caught up in the story. Your aim is to find what message the scripture has for you. Three to four verses is a good idea. Let's take an example: you'll pick a reading from St Mark's gospel at chapter 14, verses 48 to 50. The passage you have chosen is part of the narrative of the passion.

> Then Jesus spoke. 'Am I a bandit,' he said, 'that you had to set out to capture me with swords and clubs? I was among you teaching in the Temple day after day and you

never laid a hand on me. But this is to fulfil the scriptures.'
And they all deserted him and ran away.[48]

Now read the passage slowly. Don't try to work out what it's about, or puzzle over it in any way: this is not a study session. Just read it. When you have done so, put the book down and look at yourself. How do you feel having read it? What you are looking for here is an initial impression. Does the passage attract you? Repel you? Bore you? Just note your reaction, don't do anything about it, but if it does bore or repel you, don't give up because of that. There is a reason why you are reacting in that way and it is worth persevering to find out what it is.

Next, read the passage through a second time, and when you have finished, notice whether a particular word or phrase has struck you or has stood out for you in some way. Again, don't begin to analyse this, just notice it. When Laura, a young woman I know, read this passage, the phrase 'am I a bandit?' stood out for her. She was an attractive and popular woman with many friends, and it seemed an odd phrase to have struck her so forcibly. We'll consider her experience further in a moment.

Now read the passage for a third time, slowly, paying particular attention to the word or phrase that struck you. When you have finished, put the book down, close your eyes and just stay with that word or phrase, asking the Holy Spirit to show you what the good news is for you in this passage. 'Gospel' means 'good news'. Consider whether something in the word or phrase has some particular meaning for your life today. Does it remind you of anything?

Let's go back to Laura, and the strange phrase that had particularly struck her. Despite some inner resistance, she stayed with the phrase 'am I a bandit?' asking herself, why has this touched me? She found something pathetic and vulnerable in the question, coming as it does from Jesus to the band of soldiers led by his former friend Judas, who have arrived to arrest him. It indicates a feeling of being misunderstood. Gradually, Laura realised that it reminded her of a situation in her own life where a close friend who she had thought knew her better than anyone else in the world demonstrated a lack of trust that seemed to show that she didn't really know her at all. Laura had been devastated, and the breach of trust had caused a serious rupture in the friendship. Things had been patched up as best they could and Laura had genuinely believed that she had forgiven her friend, but now Jesus' cry 'am I a bandit?' echoed in her own soul: 'How could you have so mistrusted me? Did you not know me?' She realised that the wound had not been healed at a deep level, and now that she recognised this, she was able to bring it before God in her prayer, laying it open to him to receive his healing touch, and at the same time praying for her friend.

So, as you can see, this sort of spiritual reading is another form of prayer, but a more focused form than that of the contemplative prayer we have been talking about throughout this book. The two are complementary.

Spiritual reading
The other form of spiritual reading that I want to talk about is really ordinary reading, but of a book that nourishes you interiorly. In the early stages of your prayer life, you are most likely to find your inner nourishment in books about prayer and the spiritual life, books that explain to you some of the experiences you are undergoing. Or a spiritual memoir may grip your attention, as you find your food in the similar yet different journey of another person. But as time goes on and your prayer opens out into wide plains that encompass your entire life, while you will still need to read overtly 'spiritual' books, you will be astonished to discover your nourishment in the most extraordinary places, and even the most unlikely works of fiction will bring you consciously back to that centre you no longer ever really leave. One friend of mine found that the Harry Potter books drew her into prayer, as the magical world of Hogwarts reminded her of that inner spiritual world to which she could go at any moment for a meeting with her Lover who was always waiting.

Eucharist

I now want to say something about another food, the food that Jesus called the Bread of Life. In raising this topic, I am aware that I may be about to alienate some of my readers. If you are someone who disagrees with the position and rules of the Roman Catholic Church on the Eucharist, please don't stop reading at this point.

The Eucharist has, from its beginning, been paradoxically both a sign of unity and a source of division. When Jesus first spoke to his disciples about the Bread of Life, many of them found it too much to take, and they went away and followed him no longer. Yet Jesus instituted the Eucharist as a sign of his love for his friends, as a way of sharing himself with them at the Last Supper. Today, nothing has changed. On the one hand, the celebration of the Eucharist is a joyful commemoration of the union of the faithful with Jesus and with each other. On the other hand, it is a sign of division between the Roman Catholic Church and the other Christian Churches, and it even divides the members of the Roman Catholic Church itself. I will give just two examples from my own experience.

Some years ago, I followed a two-year course in spiritual direction run by a Catholic College. Among the small group of participants were several non-Catholic members. Our entire group bonded most wonderfully, and shared at a very deep level. We prayed together, sang together, ate together and studied together. Each evening, everyone attended the celebration of the Eucharist. But when the moment came to receive communion, our non-Catholic fellow-students could not receive the host. This was not by their own wish, but because of the rules of the Catholic Church. As the two years went on and our group became closer, the moment of communion each evening became increasingly painful to everyone.

In another case, a friend of mine, who had for years been imprisoned in an abusive marriage, finally left her husband. Shortly afterwards, they obtained a divorce. Some years later she met another man, one who loved her and treated and cared for her with the respect she deserved. They wanted to marry. However, because of the position of the church on divorce, they could only have a civil ceremony. Both my friend and her new husband were not only life-long practising Catholics, but also persons who had tried to live a serious spiritual life. However, because their new union is not recognised by the church, they have been told that they may not receive communion. This is a source of enormous pain to both of them.

If you have been saddened and perhaps wounded by the Catholic position on inter-communion, if you have been forbidden the Eucharist because, following the break-up of your marriage, you have found love and happiness in a second relationship, or because you are living in a loving same-sex relationship, do please read on. Although your situation may raise many issues (not least of which is how living in a truly loving relationship can be regarded as living in a state of sin) a book of this kind is not the place for a discussion of these rules. Instead, I want to look at some of the words and deeds of Jesus, as reported in the gospels – and remember, as I said above 'gospel' means 'good news'. What is the good news for those persons for whom the Eucharist is a sign of division rather than of communion?

Jesus welcomes all who come to him
First, Jesus has made it clear that we need the Eucharist; that our very survival depends upon it.

> Very truly, I tell you, unless you eat the flesh of the Son of Man and drink his blood, you have no life in you. Those who eat my flesh and drink my blood have eternal life, and I will raise them up on the last day ...[49]

Next, he assures us that we can come to him with total confidence:

> I am the bread of life. Whoever comes to me will never be hungry, and whoever believes in me will never be thirsty ... anyone who comes to me I will never drive away.[50] [emphasis added]

He urges especially those who are weighed down by any burden to come to him:

Come to me, all you that are weary and are carrying heavy burdens, and I will give you rest. Take my yoke upon you, and learn from me; for I am gentle and humble in heart, and you will find rest for your souls. For my yoke is easy and my burden is light.[51]

Jesus is above rules

From the gospels, we learn too that rules must sometimes give way to necessity.

At that time, Jesus went through the cornfields on the Sabbath; his disciples were hungry, and they began to pluck heads of grain and to eat. When the Pharisees saw it, they said to him, 'Look, your disciples are doing what is not lawful to do on the Sabbath.' He said to them, 'Have you not read what David did when he and his companions were hungry? He entered the house of God and ate the bread of the Presence, which it was not lawful for him or his companions to eat, but only for the priests. Or have you not read in the law that on the Sabbath the priests in the temple break the Sabbath and yet are guiltless? I tell you, something greater than the temple is here. But if you had known what this means, "I desire mercy and not sacrifice", you would not have condemned the guiltless. For the Son of Man is lord of the Sabbath.'

And speaking of the Pharisees, the religious teachers and rule-makers of the time, Jesus said:

They tie up heavy burdens, hard to bear, and lay them on the shoulders of others, but they themselves are unwilling to lift a finger to move them ...[52]

Addressing the Pharisees directly, he said:

But woe to you, scribes and Pharisees, hypocrites! For you lock people out of the kingdom of heaven. For you do not go in yourselves, and when others are going in, you stop them.[53]

Jesus was gentler with one Pharisee, a man called Nicodemus, a humble man who knew that he did not know everything. He came to Jesus by night to learn from him, and Jesus said to him:

Indeed God did not send the Son into the world to condemn the world, but in order that the world might be saved through him. Those who believe in him are not condemned ...[54]

Jesus did not come to call the righteous
Jesus made it clear that his mission from the Father was to seek out the lost. On many occasions, he expressed the joy that gladdens the Father's heart upon the return of a lost child to his embrace: the Prodigal Son, the Lost Sheep, the Lost Groat, are but a few of the parables in which Jesus tried to impress this truth of love upon his listeners' hearts. His behaviour reflected this truth: he mixed with those who were regarded by 'right-thinking' persons as unworthy to associate with him. A few examples of this will suffice.

And as he sat at dinner in the house, many tax collectors and sinners came and were sitting with him and his disciples. When the Pharisees saw this, they said to his disciples, 'Why does your teacher eat with tax collectors and sinners?' But when he heard this, he said, 'Those who are well have no need of a physician, but those who are sick. Go and learn what this means, 'I desire mercy, not sacrifice'. For I have come to call not the righteous but sinners.' [57]

A woman in the city, who was a sinner, having learned that he was eating in the Pharisee's house, brought an alabaster jar of ointment. She stood behind him at his feet, weeping, and began to bathe his feet with her tears and to dry them with her hair. Then she continued kissing his feet and anointing them with the ointment. Now when the Pharisee who had invited him saw it, he said to himself, 'If this man were a prophet, he would have known who and what kind of woman this is who is touching him – that she is a sinner.'[57]

A man was there named Zacchaeus; he was a chief tax-collector and was rich. He was trying to see who Jesus was, but on account of the crowd he could not, because he was short in stature. So he ran ahead and climbed a sycamore tree to see him, because he was going to pass that way. When Jesus came to the place, he looked up and said to him, 'Zacchaeus, hurry and come down, for I must stay in your house today.' So he hurried down and was happy to welcome him. And all who saw it began to grumble and said, 'He has gone to be the guest of one who is a sinner.' … Then Jesus said to him, 'Today salvation has come to this house because he too is a son of Abraham. For the Son of man came to seek out and save the lost.'[58]

God's ways are not our ways

I make no personal comment on any of the words and actions of Jesus I have quoted above. They speak for themselves. The Eucharist is our essential food for the journey. Nobody should have to go hungry, nobody should have to starve. Jesus invites us all, especially the weak and the sick. Think often of the words of Jesus that I have quoted here, and bring them into your prayer. Ask him to teach you – and to teach the church – what he meant when he said 'I desire mercy and not sacrifice.' Ask him to help you – and to help the church – to understand such a great love. Ask him to help us all to stop judging God by our limited selves. Ask him not to allow you to starve for want of the Bread of Life. And remember always that we do not know the mind of God.

For my thoughts are not your thoughts, nor are your ways my ways, says the Lord. For as the heavens are higher than the earth, so are my ways higher than your ways and my thoughts than your thoughts.[59]

CHAPTER NINE

A Friend to Keep you Company

In the Book of Tobit, we read that when the young Tobias set off on a quest for a wife, his father sent with him a companion, Azarias (who turned out to be the archangel Raphael in disguise!) to guide him along the way

The spiritual journey is a solitary one, and in the end, each of us has to travel his or her own road alone. However, it is a great thing to be able to meet up with a friend from time to time along the way, for two reasons: first, from a very human need to share with someone you trust the ups and downs that constitute the great adventure of the spiritual life, and second, in order to check that you are on the right road – especially when you come to a fork in the roadway and you have to choose which way to go next. Such a friend – an *'anam chara'*, or soul-friend, to use the lovely Irish expression, is both a comfort and an encouragement. He or she can affirm you when you are unsure, and challenge you when you are weakening.

In the Christian tradition, a spiritual director has always had an important role to play, although the level of importance has varied over the centuries. There was a time when spiritual direction was a luxury enjoyed mainly by priests, monks and nuns, and spiritual directors were mainly priests and religious. However, during the past thirty or so years, there has been a huge revival and reappraisal of this ancient ministry. Today, the spiritual director is just as likely to be a lay person as a religious, and just as likely to be female as male. And today, the spiritual director will probably have done one of the many courses aimed at fitting a person for this particular ministry in the church, a course that, hopefully, will have deepened his or her awareness of the action of God in his or her own life, and in the lives of others. He or she will have developed the art of really listening to someone else, of putting aside his or her own issues so as to devote for the time available all attention to the journey of the other person.

Today, too, spiritual directors see their role differently from that of their predecessors in previous centuries, where their relationship with those they 'directed' was almost that of master and disciple. Now spiritual direction is frequently called 'spiritual accompaniment', and the role is perceived as that of a friend rather than a master.

What spiritual direction is not
It is important from the outset to be clear about what spiritual direction is not. It is not counselling, although people quite frequently confuse the two disciplines. Counselling addresses problems in people's lives, helps them to work through them and to arrive at a solution. Spiritual direction, on the other hand, is aimed at helping people to discover how God is acting in their lives, and how to respond to and co-operate with that action. The focus of counselling is the understanding of behaviour patterns, and its purpose is to heal illness or disfunction. The focus of spiritual direction is your relationship with God, and its purpose is to integrate faith and life, and to help you to find God's purpose for you.

What is spiritual direction?
The role of spiritual director is a hugely privileged one. It permits one individual to enter into the Holy of Holies that is another's hidden life with God, and to see the wonder of God's different dealings with different people. Clearly it is a role that demands confidentiality in the same way that the role of priest, doctor, counsellor or psychotherapist does, although it is different from all of these.

If you decide to acquire a spiritual director, what will his (or her) role in your life be? Well, first it will be to really *hear* your own unique faith-story, the story of your inner life. Next, it will be to help you discover where God is acting in your life, and to assist you in learning how to respond to and co-operate with that action. Sometimes this may involve helping you to discern what decision to make at some crucial juncture in your life, but more often, it will be simply helping you to be more carefully attentive to the constant hidden movements of the Holy Spirit even in the smallest details of daily life, so that your entire life becomes rooted and grounded in Christ. And finally, your spiritual director will affirm, and if necessary, challenge you, so that you may continue on your journey with renewed courage.

Choosing a spiritual director
In your prayer journey (which is, of course, the whole spiritual journey, as what happens in prayer spills out into the whole of life) you may find it very helpful to have a spiritual director. Your local parish or diocese should be able to inform you about where you can find one. Usually, lists of persons practising spiritual direction will be available in each diocese. At the back of this book, you will also find some organisations which will be able to supply you with a list of spiritual directors.

How should you go about choosing a director? Sometimes chance, or the grace of God, will simply put the right person in your way, but if that doesn't happen, and you are faced with a list of unknown names, how should you choose? Well, first, you might try to see whether someone – the priests or sisters in your parish, for example – could recommend one or more of the persons on the list to you. If that fails, then pick a name, and see how you get on with that person. This is something you will have to do in any event, no matter how highly recommended your director may be. The same director will not necessarily suit two different people, and it is very important that there should be empathy between you. A director for whom you feel a natural dislike or antipathy will not be the right one for you. Similarly, it is important that your director feels comfortable with you. The relationship is one of trust, and it is difficult (although not impossible) for trust to flourish where one person is not at ease with the other.

Your director will understand this, and will probably suggest to you at your first meeting that you have a trial period, at the end of which you can consider together whether you are suited to each other. If your director does not make that suggestion, then you should not hesitate to make it yourself.

Practicalities

There are some practical issues which often exercise the minds of those going to direction for the first time. First, how often should you arrange to meet with your director? This is something to decide between you, but a rule of thumb would be once every four to eight weeks. Some people are happy with meetings that occur less frequently, with additional meetings factored in where necessary during times of special need.

Next, is there a fee? Again, this will be something to discuss with your director. As a rule, there is a fee, since the director is exercising a ministry for which he has been trained. Some are earning their living in this way. Others, however, may wish not to accept a fee at all. In any event, the question of a fee is unlikely to be a bar to anyone receiving spiritual direction. If your economic circumstances are such that payment of a regular fee would prove onerous, your director will more than likely be happy to continue to meet with you without payment, or for a lower fee. If he or she is not, then consider looking for someone who will.

The first meeting

So you have chosen a director and are about to have your first meeting with him or her. What can you expect?

First, as I've already mentioned, either she will suggest a trial period, or you should. Ideally, three to six meetings should be sufficient for you both to be able to decide whether you are temperamentally suited to one another. Then one or other of you should raise the question of frequency of meetings.

Payment can be mentioned now too, if you have not already sorted that out in advance.

The practical preliminaries over, your director will want you to tell her as much as possible about your faith story and where you have come to in your journey. But most importantly of all, she will want to hear about your prayer: what it is like for you, how regular it is, how long you have been seriously praying in the way described in this book. That is probably as far as you will get at the first meeting, unless of course you have some particular decision to make, and you are hoping that she will help you in your discernment. If that is so, it is as well to bring it up at the first meeting.

At all subsequent meetings, (unless you have a decision to make, in which case that may take up a large part of the time) your discussions will be about how your prayer has been since your last visit. You will also discuss any events in your life that are important to you, or that you find difficult, or that are on your mind for any other reason. This is because prayer and life are inextricably linked, the one influencing the other, and your director will need the whole picture to enable her to help you see where God is acting in your life, what he is calling or inviting you to do, and how best you can respond.

The director is also there to share your joyful discoveries along the spiritual path, and to give you support, comfort and encouragement during more painful times. She will be particularly important during that period where God begins to do the principal part of the work during prayer, because, as we have seen in chapter 7, that can be a time of confusion and bewilderment. There your director will be an invaluable guide. She will probably have trodden that path herself, but if she has not, she will have met many others who have. The way and the signposts will be familiar to her, and her reassurance that all is well will be a huge comfort to you.

A brief word about angels
At the beginning of this chapter, I mentioned the story of the

young Tobias, who was accompanied on his journey by the Archangel Raphael. So now I would like to say a brief word about those other companions on our way, the angels.

None of us can know what life after death will be like. At present, we experience life only as lived in our body: what it will mean to live without a body is impossible to imagine. But during your life of prayer, the life that has gradually been setting your spirit free, you will have had some hint of how your spirit lives. You will, as we have seen, have had the experience of inner senses, of being touched in a way that is not physical, of knowing things without the evidence of sight or hearing. These abilities will come to full flowering after our death, and it is this that will enable us to 'see' the face of God.

It seems likely to me that we will also be able to 'see' other spiritual beings, both our loved ones who have died before us, and those other beings that we call angels.

Angels have got a great press in recent years. They have come into vogue in a most unexpected way. A brief search on the Internet reveals angel therapy workshops, angel energy healing, talking with angels, angel cards, angel gifts … the list is endless. But explore some of these sites a little more, and you will find a mixture of spirituality and superstition that is quite disturbing. Some, together with certain recent popular books on the subject, give the impression that angels are there to be used and 'channelled' in order to get us whatever we want, and seem to equate these great and majestic beings with the fairies or leprechauns of our childhood, who would grant us three wishes if we managed to catch them.

C. S. Lewis' remarkable science fiction trilogy, *Out of the Silent Planet, Perelandra* and *That Hideous Strength* portrays angels in a very different manner. In the trilogy, the protagonist Ransom meets some extraordinary beings called eldila. Certain very powerful eldila, the Oyéresu (singular Oyarsa), control the course of nature on each of the planets of the Solar System. These beings are majestic and awe-inspiring, and at the end of the trilogy, we discover that they are, in fact, angels. As portrayed by Lewis, they come much closer to the angels portrayed by the Prophet Isaiah or the Book of Revelations than the milk-and-water beings of popular literature. In *Perelandra*, Lewis describes the Oyéresu or angels of the planets Mars and Venus as follows:

> Nothing less like the 'angel' of popular art could well be imagined. The rich variety, the hint of undeveloped possibilities, which make the interest of human faces, were entirely absent. One single, changeless expression – so clear that it hurt and dazzled [Ransom] – was stamped on each and there was nothing else there at all. In that sense their faces were as 'primitive', as unnatural, if you like, as those of archaic statues from Aegina. What this one thing was he could not be certain. He concluded in the end that it was charity. But it was terrifyingly different from the expression of human charity, which we always see either blossoming out of, or hastening to descend into, natural affection. Here there was no affection at all: no least lingering memory of it even at ten million years' distance, no germ from which it could spring in any future, however remote. Pure, spiritual, intellectual love shot from their faces like barbed lightening. It was so unlike the love we experience that its expression could easily be mistaken for ferocity.[60]

So what is orthodox Christian teaching on angels? The church teaches that angels are pure spirits. The Old Testament theology included a belief in angels: the name applied to certain spiritual beings employed by God as his messengers. The English word 'angel' comes from the Greek *angelos*, which means 'messenger'. In the Old Testament, the Hebrew word used for 'angel' is almost always *malak*, also meaning 'messenger'.

In the New Testament, angels are always messengers from God. They appeared to the shepherds at the birth of Jesus, to announce 'good tidings of great joy'. The angel Gabriel came to Mary to announce the conception of Jesus. An angel came to

Joseph to reassure him about Mary's pregnancy, and again to warn him to take Jesus and Mary and flee into Egypt, to escape the massacre that Herod was about to unleash on all children under two years of age.

In Matthew 18:10, we learn that the guardian angels of children always see the face of God. Traditionally, the church has always taught that each of us has a guardian angel, sent precisely to help us on our spiritual journey through life. These beings, close as they are to God, are immensely powerful, and the church teaches that we can turn to our guardian angel for help whenever we need it. As a small child, one of the first prayers I learned in school was a prayer to my guardian angel, which those of you who are of my vintage will also probably remember. As it may be new to younger readers, I will repeat it here, because it is simple and brief, and if said each morning, will serve to remind us of this friend who is always with us.

O angel of God, my guardian dear,
To whom God's love commits me here.
Ever this day be at my side,
To light and guard, to rule and guide,
Amen.

To conclude, angels are creatures of God, and to that extent, they are our fellows. But they are at a level of existence very different to ours, living as they do on the purely spiritual plane. They do not, like us, have to suffer the pain attendant on the apparent duality of body and spirit. But most importantly, they already live in that place which is the goal of our journey: the very heart of God, or 'heaven' as we often call it. We can, and should turn to these fellow creatures to ask their assistance for our own journey. We can be sure that they will help us.

CHAPTER TEN

Resting Places

In Tolkien's *Lord of the Rings*, the Hobbit Frodo travels on an epic journey. He meets with many adventures, some of them hair-raising and dangerous. But in the middle of the odyssey, he meets Glorfindel, an Elven Lord, who brings him to Rivendell, home of the Elves. There he finds rest, refreshment and healing, and is able to build up his strength and energy for what still lies ahead.

In the First Book of Kings, we find a similar story. The prophet Elijah is also on a journey. Exhausted and depressed by various events that have occurred, he sits down under a broom tree, feeling that he can go no further. But an angel brings him food and drink, and urges him to eat, saying, 'Arise and eat, else the journey will be too great for you'. And Elijah eats and drinks, and in the strength of that food he walks for forty days and forty nights, to the Mountain of God, Horeb.

All travellers need a time of rest, time out to regroup their scattered forces, replenish their provisions. You are no different. The spiritual journey is full of adventure, some of it exhausting, all of it demanding. Much of your weariness comes from the fact that you are pulled in so many different directions. You too need a time and place of rest from time to time, a time when you can store up spiritual energy for whatever lies ahead. Such times of rest are known as retreats. A retreat can be made anywhere, even in your own home, but unless you can guarantee that you won't be disturbed for a period of days, home is probably not the ideal place. What you need is somewhere quiet and peaceful, where your normal routine can be abandoned. A cottage in the country, if you have access to one, would be good. Also, many convents, monasteries and other religious institutions provide facilities for people to spend some time on retreat.

If you have never made a retreat, the thought of it may be a little daunting. 'What?' you may say, 'keep silence for several days? Oh no, I could never do that!' You might be surprised! There are unexpected riches in prolonged times of silence.

About a year ago, I went to see a film called *Into Great Silence*. It was a documentary of an unusual kind: the film-maker had exceptionally been granted permission to live for a year at the Grande Chartreuse to film the day-to-day lives of the Carthusian monks who live there. Carthusians live lives of total silence, broken only to celebrate the liturgy and, once a week, to meet together for recreation. In order to portray this life as truthfully and exactly as possible, the film-maker employed neither voice-over nor background music. The silence of the three hour long film was broken only by shots of the liturgy, one shot of the monks at recreation, and an interview with one very old monk. At the most, there were about ten minutes of sound in the entire film. For the rest, there was no story line, very little in the way of event, and a considerable amount of repetition.

What to me was very interesting was that this film played to a full house every single night, and reports from around the world were that the same phenomenon occurred wherever it was shown. The night I was there, you could have heard a pin drop in the cinema during the entire three hours. People were totally absorbed. I didn't notice anyone get up and leave.

What was the attraction? My own belief is that at least one aspect of it was that it gave the audience an actual experience of prolonged silence, something that is rarely experienced in the world of the twenty-first century. For the world of today is a noisy world. Our ears are constantly assailed by noise wherever we turn. Travelling on buses or trains, we are surrounded by the whirring and beat of personal stereos, the ringing and bleating of mobile phones, the endlessly repeated 'Hallo? I'm on the bus!' In shops, in cafes, in lifts and even in hospitals, a radio or CD will invariably be playing full blast over strategically located speakers, and even our churches are no longer the places of prayerful silence they once were. Many people feel that they can no longer support silence, and cannot bear to be alone in an empty house without turning on the television.

The loss of silence is a great loss. Silence serves, as the writer and psychiatrist Gerald May reminds us, as an emphatic reminder of mystery. In his book *Will and Spirit*, he says:

> Let those of us who are convinced that we can explain life or control our minds sit but for ten minutes in absolute stillness and all the myths will be destroyed. Thoughts and feelings rise and fall of their own accord, somehow intricately associated with breathing and with the position of one's body and eyes, levels of attention range from alertness to lethargy all beyond one's control, and qualities of perception wax and wane through a kaleidoscope of changes totally out of the range of one's own wilful influence. In these ways and many others, quiet time acts as a reminder of the mystery and the vastness that is our heritage, while simultaneously humbling us.[61]

So you may find that silence is not such a difficult thing at all, once you get used to it, but that instead, it is at the same time restful and rich.

People embarking upon a silent retreat usually find that they spend the first day or two gradually settling into the silence. It is a little like diving into the water: you dive in with a great splash, then ripples eddy out all around you, but if you stay still and just float, the water becomes calm and peaceful and supportive.

So it is that for the first day or two, the absence of external noise will make you suddenly aware of your own inner cacophony. There is even more noise inside you than there is outside. This is an alarming discovery: your mind is full of stuff, much of it junk. But, little by little, the absence of exterior noise coupled with your regular practice of prayer creates a new quietness within, a quietness in which God's voice can resound with much greater clarity than at other times. This is why people so often make discoveries during times of retreat that push them forward with great leaps on the spiritual road.

So, a retreat is more than just a spiritual rest, it is also a time of great spiritual richness. It is a time of prolonged and dedicated listening to God, of drawing nearer to him, of understanding just a little bit better who you are and where you are going. When you have once experienced the enormous benefits of a retreat, you will need no encouragement to do it a second time. I have yet to meet the person who says after their first retreat: 'Never again!'

What sort of retreat is right for you? There are several possibilities, both in terms of kind and of duration. A retreat can be of any length, from one day to thirty. However, to obtain the maximum benefit, I would recommend a retreat of at the very least three days. A week would be ideal.

There are three possible types of retreat that you might consider. You could make an individual retreat, by going off to stay in some isolated place (cottage, hermitage, monastery or convent – or indeed, as I said at the start, your own home, if you can guarantee several days of silence there) and planning your own timetable. Or you could book in for one of the many guided retreats on offer in retreat houses and centres of spirituality. A guided retreat is one in which you will be one of a number of retreatants, and there will be a regular timetable for meals, talks and other spiritual exercises. The third option is a directed retreat. It is possible to have an individual directed retreat in some places, but generally speaking, directed retreats are scheduled as part of the programme of retreat houses, and you will need to book a place on one of these.

A directed retreat differs considerably from a guided retreat. First of all, the day is less structured. Generally speaking, the only scheduled events the group will attend together are the daily Eucharist and meals. For the rest, you will be on your own – or almost. For the essential element of a directed retreat is the presence of a spiritual director. Each retreatant is allocated a director at the outset. You will meet with your director daily to discuss the progress of your retreat, and he or she will help you to explore where God is acting in your life during the retreat, and indeed, outside of it. A directed retreat can be a profoundly life-changing event.

But whatever option you choose, your retreat will primarily be a time of rest and reflection. You will have the necessary space to consider all that has happened so far on your spiritual journey, and to make plans for the continuation of the journey when the retreat is over. And above all, you will have the necessary time and silence to really listen to God's voice, and you may be very surprised indeed by what you will hear!

CHAPTER 11

Arrival

Your spiritual journey is taking you on a long adventure, leading you to the ultimate liberation of your deepest self, to the fullness of life promised by Jesus,[62] and to the freedom of the children of God. As time goes on, you will have become aware of changes in yourself: greater flexibility, a new trust in God that gives you a secret certainty that all will be well. These changes are freeing you little by little. The chains of years are falling away; doors are opening in what seemed solid rock.

The invisible cage
Where is all this going, you might now ask? Where will it end? The answer is that it will end when God has brought you to where he has always desired you to be: to the fullness of your potential as a human being. And what does that mean? It means that you will be fully alive, body and spirit in total harmony. And it means that you will be totally free. The freeing of your deepest self was only the first step in the liberation of the whole you, a liberation that you were perhaps not even aware that you needed.

In his book *Into the Silent Land*, Martin Laird tells us about an experience he had while out walking in the country. He met a man who was exercising his three dogs. Laird stood for a while admiring the beauty and energy of the dogs as they leaped and ran across the fields. Or, at least, two of them ran across the fields. The third simply ran around in circles. Their owner explained to Laird that this particular animal had been kept in a pen by its previous owner. Its only form of exercise had been to run round and round inside its enclosure. The dog was now free, but it had never come to terms with its freedom. It behaved exactly as though it were still in the pen.

Many of us are like that dog. We have all been made free by baptism, but few of us behave like free men and women. We have fashioned for ourselves imaginary prison bars, chains, masks to hide behind. But little by little, your practice of prayer has been revealing the truth to you, shattering your masks, breaking your chains, showing you the open doors. Little by little, you are beginning to expand, to move more freely and joyfully.

So, will a day come when you will be able to say, 'I have arrived'? Will there be a day when your will and the will of God will be so totally one that you will not be able to tell the difference, when, instead of dissonance there will be perfect harmony? When you will revel in total freedom, and know that you are fully human, fully alive?

Yes, that day and that moment will come. It is the day that your whole prayer life has been preparing you for and leading you towards. It is the moment when God's loving dream for you, his child, will become a reality, and you will know him at last. St John of the Cross calls that moment the breaking of the web that hides God's face and his beauty from you. It is the moment when your real life can truly be said to begin.

Most of us, strangely, call it death.

The illusion of death

Fastening on one moment, one event in the human cycle of life and calling it death, as if it was in some way the total end, is part of that great illusion – or delusion – that we spoke about at the beginning of this book. That illusion is that we are somehow separate from each other, separate from the rest of creation, above all, separate from the great source of life, that Life itself that we call God. Part of that illusion, as Eckhart Tolle points out, is that we have a misperception of ourselves, an illusory sense of identity. When most of us say 'I' or 'me' or 'myself', we are referring to an entire amalgamation of objects – body, gender, thoughts, nationality, and many more – that together, we think, are 'me'. But 'I' am much more than that. 'I' am the self that has been clothed with a body. 'I' am the self which is aware of the thoughts that pass through my mind. 'I' am not my body, 'I' am not my thoughts. Your practice of prayer will at times have drawn you into this awareness – perhaps only momentarily – but even in that moment you will have tasted the profound sense of peace that awakening to the truth of who we are brings.

As you grow in the spiritual life and as your awakenings become more frequent and more prolonged, as you emerge into the freedom of the truth, the event that we call death will gradually lose its terror. Many of the great mystics came to see that death, far from being a fearful event, was one to look forward to and to desire. In one of his most beautiful poems, St John of the Cross, living as he was entirely in the truth, expressed that truth in this way:

> O living flame of love, that tenderly woundest my soul in its deepest centre! Perfect me now, if it be thy will. Break the web of this sweet encounter, so that I may love thee henceforth with that fullness and satisfaction which my soul desires, without end, forever.[63]

What is the truth about the event we know as death? The late John O'Donoghue, poet, philosopher and spiritual teacher, gave an interview to RTÉ Radio shortly before his own sudden and unexpected death. In it he talked about ageing and death. So exciting did he make it sound, so much did he seem to be looking forward to it himself that, when the interview was over, I turned off the radio with a feeling of exhilaration and a wish that everyone could have heard him. He used an analogy for death that I had often heard before, but somehow it never before affected me with the same power with which he invested it. He said, 'If a baby in the womb was capable of understanding what birth was, if it knew that it had to leave the only life it knew, a life in which it lived in darkness and surrounded by water, if it knew that its surroundings would disintegrate, the water which was its atmosphere would disappear, and that it itself would be forced with violence through a dark tunnel, it could only conclude that this was death. It was the end of personal existence as the baby knew it.'

If death can be described as the end of personal existence as we know it, then there are many deaths in the human cycle. Birth (so far as we know) is the first one. Each stage of our development is heralded by another 'death'. The baby has to cease to exist so that the child can take its place. The child has to 'die' to make way for the adult. Right throughout our lives, cells in our body are ceasing to exist.

However, something remains unchanged throughout all of these events: the essential 'I' that is aware of all of these things happening. That is your true and deepest self; that is the self that has been set free by your practice of prayer. That is the self that will not die. So it is not true to say that you die when your body ceases to be animated by the life force. You are not your body. As the Preface for Christian Death says : 'For your faithful people, Lord, life is changed, not ended.'

Life is changed, not ended. Those of our family and friends who are no longer with us are not dead. Their life continues, but in a different way, a way we do not understand because we have not ourselves yet experienced it. But we will experience it. Your life will go on after the death of your body. That great *awareness* that is your true self will move to another stage, a stage unhampered by the illusions of the false self. It will emerge into the utter truth and will – at last! – fully taste what it truly means to be free.

Further Reading:

Beckett, Wendy Mary: *Sister Wendy on Prayer,* Continuum (London) 2006

Burrows, Ruth: *Guidelines for Mystical Prayer*, Sheed & Ward (London) 1976

Hughes, Gerald: *The God of Surprises*, DLT (London) 2008

Johnston, William: *Letters to Contemplatives*, Fount (London) 1991

Laird, Martin: *Into the Silent Land*, DLT (London) 2006

Mathews, Iain: *The Impact of God*, Hodder and Stoughton (London) 1995

May, Gerald: *Will and Spirit*, Harper (San Francisco) 1982

Silf, Margaret: *Adventuring into prayer,* DLT (London) 1999

Tolle, Eckhart: *A New Earth*, Penguin (London) 2006

Some Retreat Houses and Hermitages in Ireland

Retreat Houses
Augustinian Monastery,
Orlagh,
Rathfarnham,
Dublin 16
Ph: (01) 4958190
www.orlagh.ie

Benedictine Abbey,
Glenstal,
Murroe,
Co Limerick.
Ph: (061) 386103
www.glenstal.org

Manresa Centre of Spirituality.
Dollymount,
Dublin 3
Ph: (01) 8331352
www.manresa.ie

Hermitages
St Aidan's Monastery,
Ferns,
Co Wexford.
Ph: (053) 9366634
http://www.staidans-ferns.org/

Glendalough Hermitage,
Glendalough,
Co Wicklow
Ph: (0404) 45777
email: glendalough2000@eircom.net'
http://www.hermitage.dublindiocese.ie/home.html

Organisations which train spiritual directors

You may be able to obtain names of qualified spiritual directors from these organisations:

Anamcharadas Training Programme:
email: anamcharadas@eircom.net
Website : http://homepage.eircom.net/~anamcharadas/

Manresa Centre of Spirituality,
Dollymount,
Dublin 3.
Ph: (01) 8331352.
Website: www.manresa.ie

Notes

1. Paul Murray: 'Homage to the Void' from *The Absent Fountain*, Dedalus Press, Dublin 1991
2. Genesis 12:1-4
3. Exodus 3:1-6
4. Exodus 33:11
5.1 Samuel 3:1-18
6. Sister Wendy Beckett, *Sister Wendy on Prayer* (Continuum, London, 2006) p. 8
7. 1 John 4:8
8. John 12:1-8
9. Luke 18:9-14
10. John 8:31-32
11. Eckhart Tolle: *A New Earth* (Penguin, London, 2006)
12. John 17:22-23
13.John 5:17
14.Mark 10:18
15. St John of the Cross, *Spiritual Canticle*, translated by E. Allison Peers (Burns & Oates, London, 1988)
16. St Teresa of Avila, *The Interior Castle,* (Bantam, New York, 1998)
17. St John of the Cross, *Dark Night of the Soul*, translated by E. Allison Peers (Burns & Oates, London, 1988)
18. Ruth Burrows, *Guidelines for Mystical Prayer*, (Sheed & Ward, London 1976)
19. Exodus 33:12-23
20. Paul Murray, op. cit.
21. John 14:6
22. John 8:32
23. Francis Thompson, *The Hound of Heaven*.
24. Jeremiah 29:11
25. Luke 18:9-14
26. Romans 8:26, 27
27. Philippians 2:6-8
28. Martin Laird, *Into the Silent Land* (DLT, London, 2006), p 127
29. Exodus 32:1-20
30. I continue for convenience to use the pronoun 'he' and occasionally the noun 'God' when referring to the Divinity, as I have done throughout the book.

31. Isaiah 55:9

32. Romans 11:34

33. Job 13:15

34. Romans 7:24-25

35. John 8:54-55

36. Luke 9:35

37. John 10:10

38. Jeremiah 29:11

39. Matthew 27:46

40. Luke 24:30-31

41. Luke 24:39-40; John 20:20; 20:27

42. Ibid.

43. Ibid.

44. Martin Laird, op. cit.

45. Thomas Merton, *Monastic Journey*, ed. P. Hart (Image Books, New York, 1978)

46. Matthew 4:4

47. Hebrews 4:12

48. Mark 14:48-50

49. John 6:53-54

50. John 6:35, 37

51. Matthew 11:28-39

52. Matthew 23:4

53. Matthew 23:13-14

54. John 3:17-18

55. The tax-collectors in Israel at that time were detested, being in the pay of the occupying Romans.

56. Matthew 9:10-13

57. Luke 7:37-39

58. Luke 19:2-10

59. Isaiah 55:8-9

60. C. S. Lewis, *Perelandra* (Voyager Classics, London, 2005) pp 375-376

61. Gerald May, *Will and Spirit* (Harper, San Francisco, 1982) p 315

62. John 10:10

63. St John of the Cross, *Living Flame of Love*, translated by E. Allison Peers (Burns & Oates, London, 1988).